"Twyla has truly
Many readers will be
blessings after exposure to these words of love, beauty and devotion."

Joan Simms, RN, BSPA

"My Bible encyclopedia says prayer is the characteristic activity of the Christian life. It is a communication between man and God. That is certainly what the author portrays in her book. Twyla, in 1948 when we were just out of high school and were both entering the School of Nursing at Clifton Forge, Va., exemplified her Christian faith, and has continued to do so over many years in a nursing career and her family life. This book shows her great faith and love of God."

Betty Masters Ozmina, RN

" What a privilege to have known the author of this fine book on the power of prayer for over 50 years, first as a high school student, then a young bride, then Mother, Student Nurse, and always prayerfully with and for her Savior and Lord through whatever life brought to her and her family. Sometimes, it was great joy, other times testing and finally the death of her beloved husband, Jack. The journey here is recorded as Prayer opened and blessed all the way. May your journey as the Reader, be enriched by the author's witness shared with you. A blessing given and shared."

Ross M. Evans,
A long-time friend and Minister of the United Methodist Church

"This prayer book is unique because it is a handmade original, crafted from the pure beauty of a lifelong relationship with God. It lovingly conveys the courage, wisdom, and comforting peace available to all who include God in daily living. Read it and learn how to experience God's love and serenity even through the hardest and most difficult time. This prayer book is designed especially for you, but as you will see, through God's grace, one size fits all."

Helen Larsen, Nurse, Attorney

Ask Seek Knock

Ask *Seek* Knock
the power of prayer

Twyla Cain Wallace

Tate Publishing & Enterprises

TATE PUBLISHING
& Enterprises

Ask Seek Knock: The Power of Prayer
Copyright © 2007 by Twyla Cain Wallace. All rights reserved.

No part of this publication may be reproduced, stored in a retrieval system or transmitted in any way by any means, electronic, mechanical, photocopy, recording or otherwise without the prior permission of the author except as provided by USA copyright law.

Scripture quotations are taken from the Revised Standard Version of the Bible, Copyright © 1952 by the Division of Christian Education of the National Council of the Churches of Christ in the United States of America. Used by permission. All rights reserved.

Book design copyright © 2007 by Tate Publishing, LLC. All rights reserved.
Cover design by Janae Glass
Interior design by Lynly Taylor

Published in the United States of America

ISBN: 978-1-5988680-3-6
07.05.24

First of all, I dedicate this book to the memory of my mother, Eunice Bradley Cain, who instilled within me the beliefs that there is the power in prayer to change things, and that each human life has a purpose and is given talents by God, to accomplish that purpose. Next, I dedicate it to the memory of my husband, Jack K. Wallace, who came along at just the right time with the love, patience, support, and beliefs to help me build on that foundation and enjoy the "abundance" that makes the difference between "living" and "existing."

Table of Contents

Forewords	11
Introduction	13
What Is Prayer?	15
When Should We Pray?	19
Is Prayer Necessary?	31
Are There Conditions for Answered Prayers?	37
Does Prayer Affect God's Plan?	49
How Do We Pray?	57
"Out of the Ordinary" Happenings/Miracles?	65
A More Abundant Life	73
Power of Prayer	81
So Be It.	103
References	113

Forewords

Twyla's book touches on a very important part of our Christian Faith. Through many years of Pastoral care, I have witnessed the positive power and the positive results of prayer. I wish I had kept an accurate diary of the positive results I have witnessed through 40 years of ministry. In my own life through the years, I have felt very strongly the influence of prayer in many times of crisis and difficulties. During my military experience, I knew of the prayers of family and church, and countless numbers of times since then, I have known that many prayers were effective.

In this past year, I went through two difficult cancer operations and I can testify to great help which I received from the prayers of my family and many friends. Twyla has been a long-time friend. She is highly respected and admired, and I am thankful that she took the time and effort to share her insights. They are an inspiration and any reader will profit from her words.

Reverend Benton McKee

When I read the book on Prayer, which was written by my long-time friend, Twyla Wallace, I felt my faith renewed. Through the years, she has been an inspiration to all who know her.

In addition to being the smartest girl in our class, she has always been thoughtful of others. She was often in my home and I thought of her as a sister. She has overcome great losses in her life and her "Walk with the Lord" is genuine. How natural and right that she should choose the title, *Ask, Seek, Knock: The Power of Prayer.* She has learned first hand of the importance of prayer, and the answers from God are not a surprise to her.

How like Twyla to want to help others by sharing her experiences. Many who have gone through dark valleys as she has, would just give up, but not Twyla. She is so aware of God's presence in every part of her life. Prayer is just one part.

I count it a privilege to have had her as a life-long friend.

Mona Gray Harris McKee

Introduction

THE INTENT OF THIS BOOK is in no way for the purpose of implying piety on my part as if I feel my prayers have been answered because I met the conditions laid down in the Bible for having prayers answered. Quite the contrary is true. I am often amazed when it is so evident to me that my prayers are answered—either immediately, or over a period of time. It often strikes me with a sense of guilt and wonderment as to how it came about when actually I am so undeserving. I want to witness to everyone that God has always been there for me and has answered my prayers (in whatever was best to accomplish His purpose for me) *despite* all my unworthiness and inadequacies. If He has done it for the likes of me, He is also there—*always*—for others. I felt compelled to write this book in the hope it will encourage others to call on God for guidance daily, in *everything,* great and small. Hardly a day goes by that I don't see someone in need of a "listening ear," and the need to be given a sign of hope when they feel so much futility. Also, I'm not saying that when we talk to God, we, then, have no more problems. We will always have problems, but I hope this book will act as a guide to prayer and finding God. Just as I put things on my kitchen bulletin board, not as commands for others, but more to remind *me* daily what I must do to follow God's will—and encourage *me* when I feel I've failed—that is what I hope this book will do for others.

What Is Prayer?

What can I write that will witness to the power of prayer as I know it? I have learned from experience that prayer has great power and can make a difference. Many others also know this but may be reluctant to witness to it for fear of ridicule. Sadly, though, there are those who are unaware of this great power.

Before continuing, perhaps I should clarify my meaning of what "prayer" is. The definition I like is, "an offering up of our desires to God for things lawful and needful with an humble confidence to obtain them through the alone mediation of Christ, to the praise of the mercy, truth and power of God." (*Cruden's Concordance*) This is satisfactory to explain that our petition is for needs, and indicates faith in God's power and His mercy as He hears us. It continues that "it is either mental, or vocal—occasional; private or public, for ourselves or others for procuring of good things or removing or preventing of things evil." Further, it says that God is the only object of prayer, we must pray fervently, sincerely, constantly, with faith, and not without repentance and by the help of the Holy Spirit. That seems to be a very thorough explanation. In *The New Interpreter's Bible*, Scholar M. Eugene Boring, in "The Gospel of Matthew," says that "prayer is a particular kind of language, the language of confession," and goes on to say it is "the language that gives expression to our deepest convictions." He calls it "insider language" which may make no sense to those who "stand outside the faith."

Francois De La Mothe Fenelon says "As soon as we are with God in faith and in love, we are in prayer."

For us to pray we must have the faith that there is Someone (a higher power) there to hear it, with the power to answer. In Matthew 17, we read that even if our faith is no larger than a grain of mustard seed, nothing will be impossible for us. Surely one must have that much faith to even take the time to pray in the first place. Praying also takes humility. We are admitting that we need help—we can't accomplish the task, whatever it is, by ourselves.

It is at this point that many have difficulty, as we like to think we are capable of handling every situation ourselves. Many will go to great lengths to keep from asking for help. While independence is certainly to be admired, we overdo it when we don't ask God's guidance in all that we do. As Psalm 127 tells us, the Lord must be the overseer in all things or our labor is in vain.

Does Prayer make a difference? If not, why are we told in the Bible by writers inspired by God, to pray? Jesus prayed to God and directed his disciples to pray. His disciples later directed Christians to pray. Paul asked the Thessalonians to pray for him, Silvanus (Silas) and Timothy in their work of spreading the gospel and for protection from evil (2 Thess. 2:13; 3:1–4).

Jesus told his disciples to watch and pray that they would not enter into temptation while he went into the garden of Gethsemane when he was so sorrowful. He prayed three different times that if possible, the "cup pass from me" and finally "if this cannot pass unless I drink it, thy will be done." If prayer cannot make a difference, Jesus would not have used it, nor have directed the disciples to pray. He, further, gave the disciples what we call the Lord's Prayer, as written in Matthew 6:9–18 and Luke 11:2–13.

When Should We Pray?

Some only pray in dire need, but then, may not remember to offer a prayer of thankfulness when the "need," or emergency, is past.

We are told in the Bible that it should not be that way. Ephesians 6:18 tells us to "Pray at all times in the Spirit…" Acts 10 tells about a vision being seen by a devout man who prayed "constantly." Peter prayed "about the sixth hour," and Paul talks of "praying earnestly night and day" (I Thess. 3:10), and "evening, morning and noon" are mentioned as times to call on God in Psalms 55:17. In I Thess. 5:17, we're told to pray without ceasing, and in the next verse, to give thanks at all times because that is the will of God. In Luke 18:1, Jesus uses a parable to tell the disciples they "ought to always pray and not lose heart."

What about asking a blessing before meals? In Matthew 26:26, Jesus blessed the bread before giving it to the disciples. Paul gave thanks for the bread distributed to more than two hundred on a ship sailing to Italy (Acts 27:35). Since food is necessary for our survival, there should be no doubt about thanking God for it. Asking a blessing should be taught in the home, so that it's inbred from childhood. Some families say a blessing only when "company" is present. That's what was done in my home. When I married, however, my husband and I adopted the practice before we had children so it would be natural for them. What about when eating in a restaurant? That may need contemplation. When our children were small, it seemed that if we gave thanks at home but not in a restaurant, it may make them think it was only appropriate at certain times, yet to bow our heads and utter a prayer when eating out may call attention in a self-righteous way. This would be the opposite of praying "in secret" as Jesus directed. The important thing, of course, is to thank God for our food whether aloud or to earnestly think a prayer, as God will receive it either way.

Our little granddaughters sing (to the tune of "Are You Sleeping, Are You Sleeping Brother John, Brother John") "God, our Father, God, our Father, we thank Thee, we thank Thee, for our many blessings, For our many blessings, Amen, Amen." A blessing we taught in Kindergarten Sunday School was "God is great and God is good and we thank Him for this food, By His hand must all be fed. Give us, Lord, our daily bread." It is important that children thank God for their food and other blessings, and it may work best for them just to say a prayer in their own words, but sometimes they enjoy it more if they can sing it.

We must pray also for those who are less fortunate than we. We learn daily about people all over the world who are in need. Many are gathering bits and pieces from what others throw out in the garbage, and are without clothes and shelter. "There, but for the grace of God" could go any of us. We cannot dismiss their misfortune by blaming it on something they brought on themselves. We see people who worked hard all their lives, but because of serious, or long-term illness, or because their homes were taken away for some "progress" in society, or the greediness of "those at the top," they now have lost all for which they worked.

Only God knows why these things happen and only He is the judge if wrongs are involved. We must trust that since each is accountable to God, in the end there will be justice (in this world or the next.) What that makes us realize is that we must not take these things for granted, but always thank God for what we have and ask that those who are less fortunate will have their needs met.

Turning on a water faucet comes so naturally to most of us we never give it a thought, yet for many people that is impossible. As a child I had heard that there would always be water, but now, increasingly, we hear of its scarcity due to different causes as wastefulness, thoughtlessness, misuse, or even lack of rainfall.

God teaches us in many ways. One experience in my life gave me a new sense of my blessings and never to take these things for granted. As a co-kindergarten church school teacher, I was one of those who delivered food collected in our class to give to a poor family who lived up on a mountain. There were several children in the home, including one mentally retarded. The small house was very clean but smelled of urine since some wet the bed and the children had to sleep with each other. The family was on welfare and the husband was seldom home. (It was said he only came when he wanted money for drinking.) The mother was very thin. We learned that the only water they had was carried quite a distance up a hill. Some of the children could help. I decided then that although I had always heard "There is always soap and water to keep yourself clean," it would be awfully hard to carry water up a hill to use for drinking, cooking, laundry for a big family, scrubbing floors and keeping the family bathed (probably in a wash tub.) There also was no way to heat water except by a wood stove. I can personally relate to washing dishes in a pan, and bathing in a tub in the kitchen from water heated on the stove, when I was about twelve, and we had no electricity or indoor plumbing. What a time to thank God when that improved for me!

Do we remember to thank Him for all our modern time-saving appliances in our homes? Putting our dirty clothes in an automatic washer (instead of washing them in a stream, or on a washboard) then in a dryer; our dishes in a dishwasher; food in a microwave oven, etc—save us time—which should then be used to the Glory of God. Instead, we hurry through our "chores" so we can indulge in our own pleasures. What would happen if we prayed for guidance to use that time saved, in accordance with God's will? This is certainly not to suggest that God's will is not also for our "pleasure," but it should not be our priority.

I remember hearing that centuries ago a philosopher said that if man were relieved of having to work, there would be time for deep thinking so that all problems could be solved. Look at us today. Does anyone truly believe we are self-disciplined enough, and unselfish enough, to use the "extra" time for the betterment of mankind?

> O Lord, forgive my sin,
> And deign to put within
> A calm, obedient heart, a patient mind;
> That I may murmur not,
> Though bitter seem my lot;
> For hearts unthankful can no blessing find.
> M. Rutilius, 1604

Of course, to be "relieved of work" would not be in accordance with God's will. When He created Adam, He put him in the Garden of Eden "to till it and keep it" (Genesis 2:15.) We also are told that after God created the heaven and earth, he rested from his "work." Why, then, when we are to follow God's example, would we think we are exempt from "work"? The Bible tells us in various ways that we are not to be as a "sluggard" or "slothful" (lazy/indolent.) Proverbs 15:19 tells us the road of the slothful will have obstacles (or thorns), which, of course, would happen when we are too lazy to clear them; Romans 12:11 tells us not to be slothful in business; Colossians 3:23 tells us "whatever your task, work heartily, as serving the Lord, not men." It would seem, then, that God wants us to use the time He has given us, not in laziness, but in "fruitful" work. In Colossians 1:10, Paul gives directions "to lead a life worthy of the Lord, fully pleasing Him, bearing fruit in every good work..." As important as "faith" is (Hebrews 11:6 "... without faith it is impossible to please him...") we are told "faith, by itself, without works, is dead," in James 2:17. In 2 Thessalonians, Paul emphasizes the importance of working and not being idle, and even goes so far as to say (3:10) "If any one will not work, let him not eat." There seems to be no mistaking the importance of not sitting idly by and letting others wait on us when God has put us each here for a purpose. I believe, further, that when He created the earth and people, He intended us to be healthy and He put everything on this earth which we needed to survive, but man has polluted and made it unclean, or so refined it, that we now need supplements and means of keeping our environment as He intended it for us. I believe He put the resources in this land for our use, but we have the responsibility of using them wisely and replacing them as we use them. Some people have talents to learn the means by which to do that. Some are given talents to improve health, and some to invent things for the betterment of the earth and its inhabitants. Our gifts and blessings have not been withheld from us, so it is up to us, to whom He also gave free will, to use our gifts and blessings, as well as our time, in service to God. He also has sent His Spirit to guide us. Our bodies are the temple of the Spirit, so we must never fail to keep our bodies worthy of that. They are not for us to do with as we please.

I keep a reminder to me on my kitchen bulletin board, "Thank God every morning when you get up that you have something to do that must be done whether you like it or not. Being forced to work and do your best, will breed in you temperance, self control, diligence, strength of will, contentment and a hundred other virtues which the idle will never know." (author unknown.) We must be aware that any good we do comes from God working through us. It is not solely to our credit. "Let your light so shine before men, that they may see your good works and give glory to your Father who is in heaven" (Matt. 5: 16).

Be careful about saying "I'd just like to have time on my hands" or "I'd like to be bored." God may grant your wish. Once when I complained about having to do housework and other things as a wife, mother, and part-time nurse and wanted "relief," I got it! After several weeks of confinement with flu and complications, seeing my husband and children trying to do it all, I was thankful when the Good Lord let me get back to "normal." Another time when my husband and I complained about too many phone calls for us to have leisure time together, the calls lessened for a time, and that is not good for a self-employed undertaker whose livelihood depends on calls for his services. We reap the consequences of our actions. We have to remember that God never puts more on us than He gives us the strength to bear.

What about our health and bodily functions? Do we take that for granted? I learned not to, early in my nursing career. After seeing people either fed by spoon or by tube, not having normal bowel or bladder function—needing artificial devices, I thank the Good Lord for my blessings and ask help for those not as fortunate as I.

According to the Bible we also need to pray in order to confess. In I John 1:9, we read that if we confess our sins, He will forgive and cleanse us of all our wrongs. We must humble ourselves to admit our wrongdoing—to which no one is immune. The passage leading to it explains that we must bring our sin out of the darkness and live in the light of truth. We no longer try to hide our wrongs, we confess them to God and He forgives us. If we say we have done no wrong, we deceive ourselves and therefore make a liar of God. We must see ourselves as imperfect, but must strive to live a life more pleasing to God. We know God forgives, as in Luke 15, we read the parable which Jesus told of the earthly father who forgave his son who had gone astray, to demonstrate how our Heavenly Father forgives us when we disobey. In Eph. 4:32, we read that we must forgive others as God, in Christ, forgave us. Matthew 6:15 tells us that if we do not forgive others their trespasses, neither will God forgive us of ours. We must realize that God is always accessible to us when we feel the need to confess. The important thing is for us to be sincere, truthful, remorseful of our wrongdoing and have faith that He is there for us. Reciting a confessional with a congregation during church is not enough—although more easy than coming one-to-one with God about our less-than-Christian life—because the prepared words are too automatic to replace that personal meeting with God.

Although some feel they can confess their sins to another human being and be forgiven, no one but God has the power to forgive us of our sins. Jesus asked on the cross for God to forgive those who persecuted him. Even though one may feel better after confessing to a human being and being told their sins are forgiven and they can be at peace, that is no real assurance. God is our final judge and He can see our innermost thoughts, our intentions, and whether we are entirely truthful and remorseful. No earthly being has that power. There are some who joke about doing what they want to do and then going to confession to be forgiven. Why not confess to God—who already knows what we have done—and ask for forgiveness and guidance to help us resist temptation next time? He, alone, knows the weakness of man.

Another time for us to pray is when we see others need help. First John 5:16 speaks of intercessory prayer—interceding on another's behalf.

Ephesians 4: 1, 2, says "Walk worthy of the vocation wherewith ye are called, with all lowliness and meekness, with long-suffering, forbearing one another in love." A short prayer might be:

> Help us, O Lord, with patient love to bear
> Each other's faults, to suffer with meekness;
> Help us each other's joys and griefs to share,
> But let us turn to Thee in weakness.
> (ANON.)

In Romans 8:26 we're told we don't pray as we should so the Holy Spirit intercedes for us with God. Again, in I John 2:1, we read that Jesus is our Advocate—he speaks, or pleads, for us. This is such a comfort–to have Jesus, always perfect and sinless, plead for us, sinners, to be forgiven by God, the Father. It is also a relief that it is not necessary to have a human being intercede for us, to be forgiven. While we're told we should pray for each other, our forgiveness is not dependent on the prayers of others, because Jesus and the Holy Spirit can be depended upon to intercede on our behalf. Since Jesus shows us the way and we are to follow, then we reason that if he prays for us, we should pray for others. I know, from experience, that it is so comforting to hear someone tell me that I am in their prayers, and I, in turn, thank God for that person and ask that he/she be blessed. When a person tells me he/she wishes me "luck," I answer that I need more than "luck," I need them to say a prayer for me. We know we are interconnected spiritually and are bonded as children of God. To ask others to support us in prayer is not only a compliment to them, but also it witnesses to our faith in God.

We sometimes pass people on the street—or see them through a bus window—or even on television who look so unhappy or troubled, or we may read about them, and we can pray for them if we see no tangible way of helping them. We need also to pray for addicts and those who are mentally deficient or incapacitated in some way, as well as for their caregivers. Our military people and their families are others for whom we should pray. Here again we are saying we can pray in any place, time or position. God will hear and answer in His way and time. He also is powerful in changing attitudes and beliefs, both our own and others'. When we agree or disagree with our representatives in government, including the federal government, we need to contact them and state our views and pray about them. God has put us in a country where we have the right to express our views, and work to bring about God's will, so He expects us to take advantage of those blessings. Since we "the people" are the government, we have responsibility in providing input. (Whether it is accepted or not, we have fulfilled our duty and those who pay no attention will be accountable.) We are God's feet and hands on this earth, so we need not only to pray but work to accomplish that for which we ask.

We read in the Bible about those such as Abraham, Isaac, Enoch and others, who were directed to do things they didn't understand, but they faithfully obeyed, yet never lived to see their prayers fulfilled. We may never live to see our prayers answered, but must ask His guidance and live our lives to please and glorify Him, believing they will be answered in His way and time. The St. Francis serenity prayer reminds us to ask for "serenity to accept the things we cannot change, the courage to change what we can, and the wisdom to know the difference." We must pray for spiritual discernment so we know the difference between God's call and Satan's call to disobey what God would have us do. We must also pray to be able to discern what to try to change, that's God's will to change, so we won't be wasting time and energy on what He does not want changed.

Each day should be started with a prayer to guide us to carry out God's will and give us the strength and will to make our "agenda" in accordance with His. As we set goals for the day and for the future, we must pray that these goals are also His. Sometimes we have a day all planned out (even when we have prayed for guidance for use of the day), but there is an interruption of some sort—maybe someone needs to talk—but as I have read, that may be the most important thing we accomplish that day, and it may have been sent by God. It could also be a test of our patience or whether we really do want God's guidance as to the use of the day in accordance with His will. An old Jewish quote says we should "Do His will as if it were thine, that He may do thy will as if it were His." (*Johannine Epistles.* Pg.102.)

After the September 11, 2001, terrorist attack on our country, I heard that in the pocket of the priest for the New York City Police Department, who was killed, was a prayer which read "Let me be where you want me to be, do what you want me to do, say what you want me to say, and keep out of your way." That is, indeed, a prayer we need to write indelibly in our minds so we will seek to do that.

In answering "when do we pray," we have covered petition, thankfulness, and intercession as reasons for praying. Actually, since God is always present, all-powerful and has all knowledge/understanding—another way of saying "omnipresent, omnipotent, and omniscient"—there seems to be no inappropriate time to pray to God. Our reasons, however, must be pure. We must not pray or do other righteous acts for the purpose of being seen and rewarded by others. Jesus tells us when we do righteous acts, including praying, with the right intention—not for the sake of being seen and rewarded by others—our reward will be in Heaven (Matt.6: 1–6.)

Is Prayer Necessary?

Some might ask "Why is prayer necessary when God knows better what our needs are than we do?" In Matthew 7:7, Jesus directs us to "ask and it will be given, seek, and you shall find; knock and it will be opened to you." Doesn't this indicate we need to humble ourselves to ask God to help us? It's another way of saying we cannot do it without His help. Also, I think, in telling us to ask, seek, and knock, it tells us we need to put forth effort to bring this about. On my kitchen bulletin board (on which I stick things I *need* as reminders for myself) I have a constant reminder: "Without God's energy, I cannot, and without my effort, God will not." As an example, I know I could stay on my knees all day, praying for my house to be cleaned, but unless I get up and put forth the effort, it will not happen. Another favorite: "Pray like it all depends on God, but work like it all depends on you."

Everyone, at one time or another, needs a "listening ear". Many of those who are depressed and feel no one cares, could be helped by a loving partner or friend to whom they can talk, or "ventilate." They must know that person will continue to love and support them when they pour out their worries and concerns, even when others have fallen away. We are truly blessed and must thank God continuously if we have married someone who is there to listen intently and love us unconditionally—who knows all about us but loves us anyway. I told my husband many times that he has saved me a lot of trips to a psychiatrist. Lacking a "listening ear" at home, many are paying very costly bills to psychiatrists and therapists. This may prove helpful in some cases, but some advise the person to start putting himself before others; think of his own needs and fulfill them and he will be happier. This is contrary to God's teachings. There is no doubt there are times when we need professional help, and God has led people to be educated to provide that help, but that, too, needs to be brought to God in prayer for guidance to be led to the right therapist for that individual and to pray for God's guidance to that therapist.

The Bible tells us (John, Isaiah, and Romans) that God is our Counselor. We always need to pour out our problems to Him, whether we think they are too small or whether too large. If it concerns us, it concerns Him, because He intends us to be happy.

Sometimes we feel such anger or malice toward someone that we can't seem to let it go. We are told, however, that we must be forgiving—as God forgives us—and that vengeance is God's (Deuteronomy 32:35; Romans 12:19.)

If we do nothing to rid ourselves of that anger it can cause illness within us. It can affect our whole being. Many people are suffering from innumerable illnesses because they can't deal with the need to forgive and the anger or resentment toward another, maybe even in their own family. When one has been hurt badly by someone it is a very difficult thing to be forgiving. Sadly, there are cases when the "hurt" or "wrong" may be only *perceived* as happening. The person considered guilty of a wrong or hurtful act, may never have intended to hurt the person and may not even be aware of the person's anger or bad feelings toward him. Even if only "perceived" as a wrongful act, it can take the same toll physically and mentally on the person holding this within.

Ecclesiastes 7:9 tells us to be slow to anger "for anger lies in the bosoms of fools."

When we do not forgive, the anger eats away at us, and does great harm to us and relationships with others. We must pray to be able to use our anger constructively and to be able to forgive.

According to what I have read, Mark Twain had a unique way of dealing with anger toward another. He would write a letter to that person with everything he wanted to tell them, using insolence, if needed, and he would then put it in a drawer and never mail it. Later, as his wife cleaned out the drawers, she would destroy it. Also I have read that one can write in a journal, honestly spelling (or "spilling") out his/her anger or hurts, and that relieves the writer in a healthy way without doing harm, or incurring legal action. Let it be said, however, that there are times when the objections or disagreement, should be by "confrontation" through some communication, in order that irreparable damage be avoided.

At an early time in my life, I realized I lost my temper and got angry too much. (An Irish ancestry may have contributed to that.) I asked God to let me be rid of my temper, but later realized that there are times when we need to express our anger; otherwise we would ignore abuse and wrongdoing. Scriptures tell us in many places how God was angry with evildoers and those who were disobedient. Nehemiah 9:17 tells us that He is slow to anger. I have read, the only times that Jesus showed anger was when others were abused, but not when he was abused. We know he showed his anger with the moneychangers who were wrongfully using the temple.

We are reminded in several places in the Bible that it is our duty as Christians to be "zealous" in doing the right thing always. In I Peter 3:15–17, we're told to be prepared to make a defense to anyone who calls us to account for the hope that is in us, but to do it with gentleness and reverence, so that we keep our conscience clear and so that those who abuse us will be ashamed. It goes on to remind us it is better to suffer for doing right, if that is God's will, than for doing wrong, and we know that is what Christ did.

When we feel we have done a wrong—no matter how great or small—God is there to hear our confession and forgive us if we truly repent.

Admittedly, when we are deeply depressed or in need of guidance in making a decision and seek God's counsel, we may not get an immediate answer. He never ignores our prayers. He knows that at times we ask for what is not good for us—and as we earthly parents know, our answer is what we feel is best, whether our children understand or not; so it is with God. We must also be aware that sometimes He answers in a different way than we asked, but it is even better than our way would have been. There have been times when as I was asking for help with a decision, something came to mind I had never thought of—that's God answering.

Is prayer necessary? Yes, for all these reasons and more. God is omnipresent, so it is very necessary to our well-being, and comfort, to have such an omnipotent One to hear us any time we ask for guidance. Even though we acknowledge that He knows our needs, to ask Him for help, is also to acknowledge that we are dependent on Him for all things.

> No voice of prayer can rise,
> But swift as light Thy Love replies;
> Not always what we ask, indeed,
> But, O most Kind! What most we need.
> (H.M. Kimball.)

Are There Conditions for Answered Prayers?

In John 3:22–23, we read that we receive whatever we ask of God "because we keep His commandments and do what pleases Him." It further says that this requires us to believe in the name of His son, Jesus Christ, and love one another. In the fifth chapter of I John, we read more about loving one another as commanded and believing that the Son of God gives us eternal life. It tells us that this confidence enables us to believe that He hears us when we ask anything in accordance with His will. This sets the condition that what we seek must be in accordance with His will.

Since the condition for getting what we ask for is to keep God's commandments, we're speaking of far more than accepting God and having faith. Exodus lists the Ten Commandments from God to Moses, which all people are to follow, through all generations. That is difficult for many today to understand. A copy of a tract came into my possession, which, in a whimsical way, addresses this issue. It is called "Go Down Moses," where Moses is sent back to God by people in "modern" times, asking God to revise the commandments so they are more up to date. Each commandment is addressed by Moses to God, and He responds to each, giving the rationale, and ends with the admonishment from God to go down and say "What I have written, I have written. And don't forget—tell them I wrote it because I love them."

While many of us will admit to lying, but never to killing, the truth is that even if killing is not physical, we may break the commandment in more subtle ways. Poisonous gossip has been known to cause suicide, or to cause the death of a marriage. Oscar Wilde's *Ballad of Reading Gaol* reminds us:

> Yet each man kills the thing he loves,
> By each let this be heard,
> Some do it with a bitter look,
> Some with a flattering word,
> The coward does it with a flattering kiss,
> The brave man with a sword.

This would include things like killing someone's self confidence, or their motivation or hopes, to make themselves better. A child may fall so far behind he may never catch up or someone who had only one chance to go to college would lose that opportunity and give up. Sadly, we may all be guilty of breaking that commandment in some way.

How often does so called diplomacy, compromise, or

other strategies to "get along with, be sociable, or keep peace" actually deceive or mislead? Marriage partners sometimes keep things from each other in order not to worry her/him or not have an argument. Isn't this bearing false witness and being dishonest despite denial of those who claim it is necessary to carry on business, government, and a "loving relationship"?

Today we don't hear so much about "adultery." It's easier to call it "having an affair." Once the term was "shack up" with someone when they didn't want the responsibilities of marriage; now it's "co-habitate" or the "right to a different lifestyle." As I once heard someone put it, "The new morality is still the 'old immorality'." It's widely accepted now for unmarried couples to have children, and even single women to publicize the fact that they are having a child but do not want a male around. This seems so out of keeping with God's plan for man and woman to team up to bring a child into the world along with equal responsibilities to make a home for it. Speaking for myself, I was so thankful for a husband to share not only the physical burdens, but also the emotional and mental responsibilities, which come with parenthood. Not only are two heads better than one, but two of us needed the help of a Higher Power for guidance.

Many would also never think of breaking the commandment not to steal, but really it's common practice. What about in the workplace when unauthorized breaks are taken, when time is spent on personal calls, (and sometimes someone is trying to get a call in to the place but the line is busy) or when they think nothing of taking supplies, food, or even equipment for their own personal use—yet they accept a paycheck for full time work? Being paid for responsibilities they did not carry out is also stealing. When there is waste in electricity, supplies, or other things the consumer/patient pays for it by increased costs.

Do we ever worship, pray to, or link our destiny to some object or symbol, other than God? How often do we use His name carelessly, or less than reverently? Not only is our language today full of profanity, but "God" seems almost in every sentence in some type of exclamation. When I went to college in my late forties, I realized, as never before, how not only is obscenity common with students but also with "educated" faculty teaching the classes. I'd been taught that the four-letter words I heard were used by only uneducated or uncivilized people. (As I've read: "Profanity makes ignorance audible.") I often wonder if we are aware of how we are always in a "teaching" capacity. Children watch what we as parents, teachers, and just as "adults" do, and emulate us even when we don't know it. Athletes are often looked at as "heroes" but do not conduct themselves, sometimes, as the name implies. I read of an Olympic athlete who stopped smoking when he heard a child say he wanted to smoke because he had seen this "star" light up a cigarette. That's good.

We're told to honor our father and mother, yet we see so much dishonor, and lack of respect of some, for their parents. While we hear more today about child abuse and molesting, we also know that some will do a lot for publicity and what we often, as children, received as discipline we deserved (or later acknowledged, was deserved from a loving parent) is now often called "child abuse." Naturally, people disagree on what is acceptable as discipline, but that, too, should be guided by prayer for guidance. I feel parents have a responsibility to teach their beliefs of right and wrong and then it is the children who are accountable for how they use that teaching. Understanding certainly comes best after the experience of parenting and having to make the decisions necessitated by the responsibility for another's life.

When marriage takes place, of course, we may acquire another set of parents. That can be good or bad. We can't choose our mate in accordance with whether we like his/her family, but we may not be compelled to live with them. We still must honor them because marriage unites husband and wife as "one," so they become our parents as well. Since my mother was deceased, I felt very blessed with "parents-in-law" I could honor very easily, and tried to make them happy with their son's choice of a wife. I often sought, and received, advice from my mother-in-law and was very thankful for her. We must remember that had it not been for her, we would not have our mate, and should honor her as our own.

It is too bad that through the years there has been an unbecoming stereotype of "in-laws," especially mothers-in-law and maybe sisters-in-law, so that there is at least one count against them when marriage occurs. There is already the expectation that there is going to be trouble. It's like the stereotype of the stepmother portrayed in fairy tales. It sometimes makes it difficult for the mother of a son or daughter who continues to love that "child" but is made to feel unwanted and not a part of the family. So much is gained when the family just extends as another is added. We can learn so much by accepting each other, and the grandchildren benefit if allowed to. Of course, the same is true for parents accepting those chosen by their offspring. Admittedly, there are those who are so selfish, or jealous, that a good relationship seems impossible. If God is truly accepted into the family, then there should be a happy relationship with parents honored on both sides, and children will learn to honor their parents and the parents of their parents. As we are aware, it is often easier to love "everybody" than to really be tolerant, patient with faults, and love and accept those closest to us.

We can do this analysis with each of the Ten Commandments and find we come up lacking, but thanks to God, He is the ultimate Judge of our obedience and will determine if we have true salvation and have met the conditions for having our prayers answered.

I believe when we pray, our motives must be right and they must be unselfish. I learned this in my own life. My father, at about the age of 49 or 50, began to show signs of a mental illness, attributed to his service in World War I, and when I was eight years old, my mother was forced to admit him to a Veterans' Hospital in our state. Our prayers were always that he would get well and come home to us. I would pray he would come home so he could be my daddy, and we could do things together as before. I also wanted my mother to have him back. She worked very hard at cleaning for others and earning little. My only sibling, a sister ten years older than I, who was a student nurse, was killed in a car wreck by a drunken driver, before she was twenty. Ironically, the driver was a former patient of hers in the hospital. He had been almost killed at that time, and some said it was a "miracle" he survived.

Upon graduation from high school, I entered a three-year hospital based nursing program. In the course of my psychiatric studies, I began to learn, and was told by those caring for my father, that it was not likely he would ever be able to leave the hospital. He had been moved to a long-term Veterans' Administration hospital in another state not long after being admitted initially. I continued in my prayers for him to come home to me. Although I had always believed my prayers would be answered, my scientific learning made me have second thoughts. Also my visits reinforced them.

I began to change my prayers, just to let him know he was loved and had not been abandoned. In the beginning, doctors had advised that he not be told of my sister or mother's death as he may not be motivated to come home, and may become more depressed. In fact, he had expressed to my mother on a visit that if anything happened to any of his family, he did not want to come home.

After my marriage, I began to tell him in letters about these facts, without details, so he knew the reason for no visits by them. I felt the truth might help him more.

After having been institutionalized for seventeen years, my husband and I brought him home with us. He was able to stay with us and relatives, and also to live by himself in an apartment in a place near his old home place where he had an older brother whom he could visit and help with the garden and farm.

I know without a doubt, that prayer, over all those years,

changed from a selfish prayer of wanting him home for me, to praying for what he needed, brought him home. God answered my prayer at the best time in all our lives. He had had no treatments, nor medications, for years so that is not the reason for his "recovery." He was able to hunt and fish as he'd always loved to do with my mother's brother, who had long given up the hope of ever seeing him again, much less going back to their old habits.

He had always loved the outdoors and loved to walk in the woods, hunt, fish and garden. He would put in a large garden on a hillside and then compete with a friend, who lived up on the mountain beyond us, to see who could grow the largest potatoes. (My mother canned a lot of vegetables from the garden.) I can recall as a small child how he would sit on a log, up at the top, and look over his garden and would encourage me to come up and sit with him, which I did. He would tell me about the animals and what kind of trees were around us. I remember his cutting off little birch branches for me to chew on the birch, and I found it good. Once a snake started up on the log and he quickly grabbed a branch, or something nearby, and beat it off. It is not surprising that he loved working with wood and was a very good carpenter and painter—in fact he was employed for a time with a building contractor. He made me a little ironing board that folded up just like a real one, and a little wooden rocking chair which I still have, and our granddaughters sit in when visiting. He was an early riser and an energetic worker. He would wake me sometimes early in the morning telling me the sun was going to beat me up. I didn't really care that it did!!!! He was a very gentle man, and I don't recall him ever disciplining me or my sister. (Our mother certainly did, though. She believed in using switches and I remember feeling those many times {all deserved, I'm sure.} Today if that happened—or less—it would be called "child abuse," but I knew her discipline was a part of her love.)

It was so enlightening to see a person who, after leaving the grounds of the institution, (very insecure and afraid of getting lost when my husband and I would take him out, even on the grounds) now saw how the highway system and other things had changed since being hospitalized seventeen years before. He would call me to come and see things like the big tractor- trailers carrying so many cars. It was like looking at the world through a child's eyes, since there had been so many changes in all those years. He loved getting up early in the morning and sitting under our trees listening to his little radio, and greatly enjoyed using his camera to take pictures and playing with our little ones (born after he came home). He would buy pretty ruffled dresses for our little girl. (As a father of three little girls—although one lived only about four months—he seemed to know more how to relate to them, but he also loved and gave a lot of attention to our little boy.) As our son got older, he would talk to him about baseball which he loved. We owned seventeen acres of land, and he could walk out in the woods and even kill a rabbit on occasion. He sometimes would pick wild flowers to bring in. On one occasion he came in with really large peaches from a tree we didn't know we had, which had come up in an area where we had dumped our trash, including peach seeds, and there he had found a little tree producing peaches. He really delighted in nature.

His return after so long really gave me an indelible faith in how prayers with unselfish motives are answered. While I was told by relatives and others that he would never come home, I never stopped praying and saw it answered at the time that was right for us all, according to God's plan. In retrospect, I do not believe it would have "worked" if he had come back earlier. As it also "happened," the funds, small as they were, from the government while he was confined, provided for my "keep" while staying with my aunt, uncle, and cousins, as well as for me to go to nursing school. He got home to no responsibilities for family or job, and received from the government enough to provide his needs and pleasures, at the best time of all. It was amazing to everyone. It's strange how we pray for something and then are amazed when it comes about! (Oh! Ye of little faith!) It also re-emphasizes the importance of having right motives, not selfish ones, for praying.

In the Gospel of Luke, Jesus addresses issues of persistence in prayer, and in Matthew, he is concerned about intentions. In the 6th chapter of Matthew, he tells us we must not pray for the reason to "be seen by men." In other words we are to pray for valid reasons, not for praise from others. He says if we do that, we receive our reward from men and will not receive it from God. We are to pray sincerely. In the Lord's Prayer, as we ask for forgiveness for our sins "as we forgive those who sin against us," it really means "to the degree that we forgive others," not "because" we forgive others. We know we are forgiven unconditionally by God as we accepted his gift of atonement; but it is difficult to always forgive those who have "trespassed" against us.

We often must pray for help to do that. While He tells us we will be forgiven as we forgive others, it does not mean He will not discipline us for our disobedience.

Somewhere I've read the reminder that we must not confuse "the fatherhood of God with the daddyhood of God." While we don't like to think about it, because it's so much easier to think about His love and patience with each of us, we're told by both Jesus and Paul that the wrath of God is a real and awesome fact: Matt. 22:13; 25:10–13; 30; Rom. 1:18; 2:1–9.

We know Christ died for our sins and as we accepted that gift, we are not made to die for our sins, but He would not be the right kind of Father if He let us get by with all our misdoings. We suffer the consequences of our wrongs, and that should teach us to be more obedient to His ways. I believe that even though we know we are forgiven, some of the consequences which may result are feelings of guilt which continue. Guilt feelings, of course, is the remorse we need to feel in order to be forgiven. We must not, however, allow our feelings of guilt to interfere with our work to go on and try to live a more godly life. We could stay on our knees all day asking for forgiveness and guidance to do better in the future, but unless we get off our knees and go about our work, we do not accomplish God's plan for us.

In summary, Matthew 6:1 gives us good advice for serving God in the right way: "Beware of practicing your acts of piety (righteous acts) before men in order to be seen by them for then you will have no reward from your Father who is in heaven." It is my belief that right motives are a part of the conditions for which our prayers are answered.

We know, ultimately, however, it is really God's grace and love which is why our prayers are answered, and He considers each one individually, because He knows us as no one else does. It is not anything we have done to "earn" answers to our prayers.

Does Prayer Affect God's Plan?

We might ask if prayer could prolong a life. "Predestination" might be cited to mean we are to die at a certain time no matter what. Throughout the Bible we learn that God is love. He loved us so much He sent His son to show us the way we could all be saved instead of perish in Hell. Often we hear that a tragedy was God's will. A minister, talking with my husband and me, once asked how anyone could think a loving God planned for a child to let loose of its mother's hand and run out in front of a vehicle right before her eyes. He had a very good explanation, similar to that written in an exemplary way in *The Will of God* by Leslie D. Weatherhead. Also I have had a great deal of help in understanding, from *A Bird's Eye View of God's Plan*, by John R. Church, DD.

From all my teachings since a child, I feel strongly that God has a Plan for the whole universe and each one of us has a part in that Plan. I believe every person who comes into this world is *given* certain talents to fulfill that purpose. He can choose to follow God's will and develop those talents or choose not to develop the talents. We must each pray for Spiritual discernment to choose what the will of God is. They may be talents we could never suspect we have, but you become aware you can do something more easily than something else and enjoy it very much. I believe if we develop the talents and choose the "calling" God has intended for us, we will be happier than otherwise.

In the literature, we find that Florence Nightingale believed that she, as well as everyone else in every vocation, had a role to play in God's plan. When the person performed the job well, divine perfection was achieved. She considered the job of shopkeeper, lawyer, merchant, statesman, doctor, and others who labor, equally sacred with that of the priest. We should always include God in whatever job we have, and that should be obvious to those with whom we have our daily dealings.

If we choose a career for the purpose of making the most money or for fame, we probably will be unhappy. This, of course, is not to say your "calling"—what God intends you to do—will not make you rich or famous, but it would come about—not with the motivation to become rich and famous—but more as a "by-product."

We know part of God's plan for each of us is to have only a certain length of time on this earth—otherwise there would be no space or resources for new births with talents to meet the ever-changing world.

As a nurse, I have often heard a doctor tell the patient

or family that there is no more that can be done and they must accept that the patient will not survive. Yet, I have seen individuals, or sometimes "prayer groups," pray sincerely for that person and he/she recovered, maybe even lived for years. Did prayer do it? I believe so. I believe it happens even when we may not believe it will. It seems very possible from what I have read that while God's will and Plan will never, in the end, be defeated, there are actions which can delay it. In *The Will of God* it is called God's "ultimate will" which will never be defeated, but there is also God's "intentional will" and His "circumstantial will." God never intends for us to be hurt or unhappy, but since He gave man free will—and there is evil in this world—also laws of nature which won't be changed, His intent might be altered. Then things happen because of circumstances. It was not God's intent for the child to be run down by the car. When the child ran in front of the car, the law of nature would be that the force would kill the child, as when one falls from a high window and hits the cement below, the law of nature would not be changed.

Also, God's "ultimate will" can be brought about in a different way than intended, because of circumstances—sometimes evil—but in the end His overall/ultimate Plan will be achieved.

In the Bible, we're told how God allowed Job's faith to be tested, so if a God-fearing man like Job can be tested, why can we not also expect to be tested at times? Sometimes our suffering results in helping us to be more disciplined and it can result in bringing forth strength we never knew we had, and our faith is tested. Death of a loved one can also bring forth these virtues in us. As we look back, we often see that it was a part of God's Plan. He always gives us the strength to bear what happens to us.

When at fourteen, I lost my mother, only 46 years old, I could never understand why God took her whom I needed so much. I felt it would have been better for Him to take me and leave her as she was such a good Christian, and I felt her prayers were more powerful than mine, and she was more worthy of life than I. Later, I realized that if she had lived, I probably would not have left her alone, to go into nursing school. Also, as I'd tried to help her when she suffered bad attacks of asthma, I more deeply wanted to learn how to help sick people. God, at the same time, put me in the care of loving aunts and uncles. No one could ever take her place, but I was never without kind care, and learned to live in a very active household made up of several people. It was like having brothers and sisters. I had always wanted an older brother so that worked out too. Because of the deep Christian foundation my mother had given me and how she lived, I was able to accept it all even though I didn't fully understand. She had given me the faith to believe all things work together for the good of those who love God. I feel deeply it was God's Plan for me to be a nurse to help others, and He gave me the talents to carry out my purpose in His Plan and the opportunity to develop them. More than fifty years have been spent in various areas of nursing, from direct care and supervisory care, to teaching nursing in both hospital and college programs. I have enjoyed it despite much stress as a natural part of the occupation. I realize, too, that what I learned in nursing helped me in every other aspect of my life. As God let me be a wife and mother, homemaker, worker in church and community and in other areas, my nursing came to my aid.

My faith in the power of prayer has been greatly deepened by so many demonstrations of people improving when there seemed to be no hope. Private duty nursing for twenty five years gave me my greatest joy as I worked directly with the patient giving what is now called "holistic" nursing as the physical, mental and spiritual needs are addressed. In all I did for the patient, prayer was offered to God for guidance in providing the needs of this patient in accordance with His will. When patients would ask for me to pray with them, I did. When present at the death of some patients, it was a lesson in what waits beyond as they might talk of seeing a bright light, or of such beauty, or sometimes hearing music or singing, or talk to people who had preceded them in death. Nursing gave me such great lessons in so many things, I know it was what God meant for me. Not the least of these lessons was to be thankful to God for health and other things I may otherwise have taken for granted.

Praying for others, intercessory prayer, has been previously discussed and, since we have been thus directed in the Bible, is another reason to believe that prayer changes things; or why all the directions to pray for others? Also we are told in Hebrews 7:25 that Jesus lives for all time to make intercession for those who draw near to God.

In a recent event, I feel sure that prayer made a difference in a member of the Sunday School class I attend. I feel also that it was for the purpose of teaching a large number of people, not only in our class, but even beyond our church, that miracles still happen. This middle-aged lady was very active in the church and community, the mother of grown children, and the increasing disabilities of her husband's father made it necessary for him to depend a great deal on them for help. She suddenly began to have difficulties in speech, reading, and doing the activities of daily living. She was diagnosed with brain cancer. As she continued to come to church with the help of her husband, it was devastating to see her deteriorate. It was the priority of our class to have prayer for her, both in class and individually. A "prayer quilt" was made and as people in the church, and church circles, would say a prayer they would tie a knot in the long threads sewn into the squares. She did undergo chemo and radiation and need lots of help, which was mostly provided by friends who volunteered. Soon she started to amaze everyone who saw her, as she continued to come to church and go to other activities, wearing a hat, and at first limited by a wheelchair, but later walking and making unbelievable progress. She is back to being able to help care for her father-in-law, walking alongside him, as before, when they come to Sunday School and church. While her life may still not be back to normal, and may be shorter than hoped, it has been a valuable lesson to all that prayer—as well as her faith—has made a difference. All things are working out better than it looked in the beginning. We have all been inspired by her, and her husband's, great courage. Her husband has, likewise, been an inspiration of what love can do and will tolerate when it is a union of Christian love.

I think this is evidence that prayer is powerful enough to change many things in our lives or else there would not be so many examples in the Bible telling of its use and advice to pray. We know from the Bible that we are to help all others however we can, and sometimes it is the *only* way we can help someone, as in foreign countries or other situations. Even when one is physically, or financially, unable to help another, a prayer can be said.

Much time and effort would be lost if prayer makes no difference.

How Do We Pray?

Since prayer is the act of communicating with God, then how do we do this? In communicating with humans we verbalize, use sign language, write, e-mail, or use the telephone. Even that takes faith because some of the "mechanics" of any of those things can fail. It's different to communicate with one unseen, and even more difficult when we don't receive some sort of immediate answer.

One definition of prayer tells us we can communicate with God through word, thought or spirit. This gives encouragement over the regulations not permitting prayer in school. Unless we are stopped from thinking, we cannot be stopped from praying through thought. (Granted: children may need a scheduled reminder and given an opportunity to pray—or not.)

Some believe that praying can be done only in certain positions, or places, or only by using certain objects or rituals. Some believe there is no need for a type of "formality," or actual asking, but merely by being a Christian it's understood. They acknowledge and do as He wills, so don't need to ask for help. They also say God knows they're thankful. They may be using Matt. 6:8, where we are told that God knows what we need before we ask Him. Yet, we're told in many other places, as cited previously in John 15:7, to "ask whatever you will and it shall be done for you" and in James 1:5, 6, that we can ask for wisdom, and if done in faith without doubting, it will be given us. Matthew 7:7, 8, as mentioned before, tells us to "ask—seek—knock… for everyone who asks receives…"

My mother taught me about prayer early. She taught me just to talk to God and ask, or thank Him, in my own words, and she would pray beside me as we prayed to let my dad "get well and strong and healthy and come home to us." It seemed etched in my brain. She also stressed the importance of thanking Him for all we had. Of course, as many children did then, I learned the prayer:

> Now I lay me down to sleep
> I pray the Lord , my soul to keep,
> If I should die before I wake,
> I pray the Lord, my soul to take.

While I didn't exactly understand it, because the way I said it was "Now I lammy down to sleep" and I wondered what a "lamb" had to do with it, but still I felt comforted in that. It makes us wonder, as we mature, if we should better explain what we are teaching; however, it made no significant difference to me at that time.

When we said a blessing at meals, we simply said it in our own words.

No humility is required of us if we take the position that God already knows what we need/desire without our admitting we need His help.

In Matt. 6:5—14, we read that we must not pray for the sake of being seen by others and therefore receive some sort of praise for our piety. This embraces all that we do—what are the real motives behind what we do? Any time something is done (even if it meets a great need) for the sake of getting a reward or praise, or with malicious intent, we gain nothing as far as God is concerned. Sometimes we see someone hailed as a great philanthropist because of large amounts of money to a particular cause. Did that person accumulate his wealth by overcharging people for his services or merchandise, or by some illegal method, or taking advantage of vulnerable people? What about the person who undercharges the "going rate" or gives freely of his services/merchandise so he never accumulates enough to become a philanthropist? We're told in the Bible that we must not conform to the world in order to please our fellowmen. It is God who judges us, and He can see what is in our heart—our real motives.

The Gospel of Matthew tells us that we are not to heap up empty phrases, thinking that God hears only those who pray long prayers. However, "their many words" does not necessarily mean the length of prayers (because Jesus prayed long prayers) but it has more to do with phrases which seem to deny our faith that he hears our prayers. The Lord's Prayer is, then, given as an example for us to pray.

Each person must answer the question for himself on how to pray. We have the Bible as a guide and then must interpret it to the best of our ability, and trust that God hears us however we do it, as long as our intent is right.

There are the times I'm most desperate and get on my knees to pray (it may be also for when I am most thankful for some blessing), and it may be aloud—when I'm alone. Nothing distracts me, and I can hear myself praying. It is not always a plea, but may be an acknowledgement for something that could have happened only by God's doing or an answer to a fervent prayer. There are many times when I think a prayer as I drive along. It also is often necessary to pray in our minds when others are around, or as we busily do chores and ask for help or give thanks. I usually pray in bed but must be careful when I do it at night, that I don't fall asleep or allow myself to be distracted. (Is that Satan doing the distracting?) We need to remember to pray in the morning for guidance to carry out God's will for the use of the day, and also for thankfulness for a new day and new opportunities, and that we live in a free land. For me, it is necessary to mention the name of each person I feel needs help, and those who have requested prayer. I also ask His help with things I feel I must do that day. I ask that He will help me live a more godly life as a parent, as a worker in whatever causes or "projects" to which I'm committed, and for forgiveness when I've been disobedient. Believing Satan is always there to tempt us, I ask God to help me resist those temptations. When I feel I need acceptance by someone meaningful to me, or I may have been thoughtless, I ask for a way to remove the "wall" and help me be more mindful of other's needs. It seems necessary for me to spell out all these things, even though I know He already knows where and who needs the help. I feel so much better for having mentioned all these individual matters. As you can imagine, my morning prayer takes an hour or more. I also ask His guidance for our leaders, national and state, county, and city/community-wise. When I don't pray in that way, I feel my day has not started right. It's part of my "normal" routine along with morning devotions, proper nutrition, exercise, and recreation. This, I guess, may show my insecurity, but God knows and accepts my reason, whatever it is. My husband used to thank Him as soon as we turned into our driveway, after we had been out. It remains a habit for me now that I am without him.

At night we again need to thank Him for our safety and His guidance during the day and for peace and safety through the night. Whenever we pray, we know we just talk simply like we talk to our friends. Some say they don't have any idea how to pray, but since they talk to get their needs met in daily living, that is no excuse. We hear a lot of people these days, using the exclamation "Oh, my God" for any number of things. Do they use His name also at times when it is meaningful?

Certainly, there is no one place we have to pray. We go to church to praise and worship God with our songs, prayers, offerings, and service, but that should not stop when we leave church. We pray and worship Him with our services at home and in the workplace as well. A cartoon I have posted, says it all when the little girl tells her family as they leave the church that "Grandma says this is where our real religion starts."

I feel certain that I never would have gotten through my studies in school—including nursing, college, and the massage program I took in my sixties—had I not prayed for help. I asked God's help in all my tests and in my clinical experiences, knowing it all depended on God and working at it as I knew He intended for me to do, and I got through them all. Admittedly, however, my husband not only provided encouragement but also did so many things that many husbands would never think of doing, to give me time to study and attend classes. He never hesitated to cook, clean, or whatever, so I could be free to further my studies. (That was also true in being a father. He got up at night with our little ones just as I did, and often he had to be out at night for our funeral business. That did not stop him from carrying out his responsibilities as a daddy.) He felt I was meant to teach nursing after our children were older. I continue to feel very indebted to him for my accomplishments in becoming educated with a master's degree in education when nearly fifty years of age. It was a very proud day when I graduated from college the same year as my son graduated from high school. Our daughter was in college studying music. I wrote out my thanks and gratitude in a Certificate of Appreciation, prepared by our very artistic daughter, spelling out some of the things he did, and that he was a Master at keeping his sanity and sense of humor as he sometimes served as father and mother, to allow me to pursue my education.

Somewhere I read "God will work *with* you but not *for*

you." In other words, He has given us the opportunity and the ability, so expects us to put out the effort to help make it happen. I pray for help in my cooking, baking, and homemaking as I need His help, and know that what concerns me, concerns Him, including what many may consider too small to bring before Him. Often while working, I will misplace something, or will start to do a task and cannot find something that I need in order to do the task, and I will spend so much time looking, that it becomes very frustrating. Living alone now, I am more frustrated because I feel sure I put it in a certain place, and I will say "God, please help me find (whatever.)" So many times I will find it in a spot I have looked before, or maybe a place I would not have suspected. Strangely enough, I have reluctantly mentioned this to close friends and found they, too, have had this happen. Does God answer prayers which have no big necessity involved? I think He does, since the intent is for good, and because it concerns one of His children.

Since many people are unable to assume a certain position to pray, we know it is not required by God. Words such as "fervently," "sincerely," "steadfastly," are used throughout the Bible (Colossians, Psalms) to describe how we are to pray—reminding us that attitude is very important in prayer. In James, we're admonished to pray with faith; in Psalms, "not without repentance," and in Romans, "by help of the Holy Spirit." As for "position," in Mark 11:25, "standing" to pray is mentioned; in Matt. 26:39, Jesus "fell on his face" to pray that "if it be possible, let this cup pass from me…"; Acts 21: 5, "kneeling down…"; 2 Samuel 7:18, "…King David went in and sat before the Lord…" to pray;

Daniel 6:10, "got down on his knees three times a day to give thanks...." "Position" and "place," as we see, are not as important as attitude and motive for praying. In *The New Interpreter's Bible*, "The Gospel of Matthew," M. Eugene Boring makes an important point when he says "Prayer is sanctified when addressed to God in whatever space is used, while prayer that means to call attention to the one who prays is unacceptable anywhere." We might want to add to that also, "any time."

"Out of the Ordinary" Happenings/Miracles?

RE THERE MIRACLES today as those we read about in the Scripture? (Heb. 2:4, John 2:11.) Was my father's recovery—of which I've written—a miracle? I count it as such. The dictionary defines "miracle" as "an event that is contrary to, or independent of, the known laws of nature," or "manifesting divine intervention in human affairs." Since my father's inactivity and withdrawal from socialization had caused premature hardening of the arteries, a progressive process, and he was receiving no medications or therapy, there is no scientific evidence to explain an improvement in his mental condition after several years of status quo. His improvement was independent of the laws of nature and as the prayers of my mother and me sincerely petitioned God for his recovery, there was certainly "divine intervention."

I believe we witness miracles quite often but are reluctant to admit, or recognize, it. Too many just attribute them to "coincidence" or "luck." We do sometimes hear "miracle" mentioned in cases where there is one survivor in a plane crash, shipwreck, or whatever, when only one survived and all the others died; or when someone's found alive after a storm or earthquake has reduced the area to rubble. We even hear it when a newborn infant or disease-ridden person survives against all odds. How many times, however, do we also consider it a miracle when in our daily driving we narrowly escape being sideswiped or in a wreck on the highway? Sometimes we see a terrible pile-up of cars in which we may have been involved had we left a few minutes earlier. When highways are slick or icy and we lose control, but for "some" reason our car stops just short of collision with a pole or another car, or in our rush we dash out into traffic taking a chance—over-dependent on our cars—but we "make it," do we think it was just "luck" that saved us? It is God to whom we owe our thanks, not "luck," or our car, or our driving skills! Again, it was "divine intervention," and if we said a quick prayer for safety in these events then it's more evidence of answered prayer. We need to be mindful of these close calls and why we were spared. There must be more work for us to do in God's name.

Another event in my life is "out of the ordinary" or a "miracle," as I think of getting back a ring my mother had lost many years before.

As my father began to respond to the visits my husband and I had made to him in 1955 at the Veterans' Hospital and to my letters following, he wrote me to get the valise he had taken with him when he had been admitted (in 1938.)

I recalled having received the valise with some of his personal articles in it when I was living with my aunt and uncle and going to school, and putting it in the back of a closet. It was among things we would move out yearly to do "Spring cleaning" and replace, but since then I had gone into nursing school for 3 yrs. and then had been married for four years. I went to my aunt's and found it, to my great surprise. I followed his directions: "In the bottom of it you will find a little slit and inside that, you will find your mother's engagement ring in a piece of newspaper." I had no idea that even if he remembered correctly, it would still be there after all the years. It had been in two different hospitals (as he had been transferred about a year after admission to the V.A. hospital in the state where we lived, to another V.A. hospital in a different state, where he had stayed for about a decade before I received it.) To my amazement, there was the engagement ring. I had heard my mother berate herself through the years because she had lost it. My father said she was always taking it off and laying it on a shelf above the sink when she put her hands in water. He had warned her she was going to lose it, so decided to "teach her a lesson." When he saw her take it off, he hid it and never told her about it. I was sorry she had died regretting the loss of her ring. I felt it was a miracle to still be where he had put it. He said I was to take it, have it cut down to fit me, and wear it. My husband suggested I wait and make sure he didn't change his mind. When he came home, however, he went with me to have it made to fit me, and I proudly wore it for years until the setting broke and couldn't be repaired. God is so good to us with so many unexpected blessings. It made my father as happy that he could make me that gift as it made me to have it, and I feel sure my mother in Heaven was happy about it.

We read in the Bible of visions being used at times to declare God's will for a person. Through a vision, "Saul," a man who dealt cruelty to Christians, became "Paul" the apostle, an instrument of God's will, whose letters in the New Testament continue today to teach us. Abraham, Moses, and others in the Bible were visited with visions from God. Today we also read of people seeing visions. When someone is near death, we sometimes hear them relate the beautiful scenes they are seeing, or beautiful music they are hearing. I also have heard them call out names of people who have already left this world, and maybe even talk to them. What I have witnessed has always been a peaceful happy experience for the person, not fearful or morbid.

Do we sometimes get messages from God when we are praying and sometimes in our dreams? There are times when, in the middle of asking for help in solving something, I suddenly get an "idea." I feel that's a message. Those who meditate must also have similar revelations.

An event in my teens had a lasting effect on me regarding God's personal intervention into our lives when we need Him.

I was so devastated at age fourteen when I lost my mother. Even though I was more mature and able to do more than most at my age, I was very dependent on her (and insecure) after losing two members of our family of four. There also had been the loss of my mother's younger brother and sister just a few years before she died. All of this added to my insecurities and concerns about life and why things happen. I could see no reason why my mother, whom I needed so badly, and who was a good Christian, should be taken by God. I missed her so much at night and would awaken to sadly face another day without her. I was living with my uncle (her brother) and aunt. My cousin, two years older, shared her room with me and it was very nice. I had never before had a bed to myself because my mother and I (and even my older sister, while at home) had shared the same bed. My cousin was nice enough to allow me to sleep with her until I could get over the initial shock of being alone.

One morning, however, I awoke with an unusual sense of happiness and relief—as if a burden had been lifted from my shoulders. I thought my mother was with me. Then I realized that my mother had appeared to me during the night. It seemed more real to me than a dream. She had looked so healthy and happy. I told her I was so glad she was there; I thought she had died. She told me she had been sick for a long time, but now was well and that I must quit worrying about her. It was such a revelation to me, it still brings a sense of peace even as I recall it today. I knew, beyond a doubt, that my mother was in Heaven with God, and much better off than if she had continued to live on earth. While I still missed her, I felt more peace about her and why God took her.

I'm sure that served many purposes. My mother's "visit" had removed some of the grief for my loss. (She had simply gone to sleep after a doctor gave her a medication by injection, for relief from a severe attack of asthma, and I fully had expected her to awaken, not die. An aunt had been called by a neighbor, and she had persuaded me to lie down beside my mother in bed since it was getting late.) It verified my belief that the grave is not the end, because she was alive and looked so happy and healthy. It also gave me faith that God loves us and is there for us, each one. I felt better about going on with my life and wanted to make her proud of me.

We all would be in a sorry shape if we received what we "deserve." We know it's God's grace—His love and mercy—through which He continues to give us another chance. As sinful as man was (and continues to be) to Jesus, he prayed for their forgiveness after they nailed him to the cross.

The practice of righteousness and saintliness certainly are not the reasons God chooses leaders or agents in His work. As we read about some of the Biblical characters and their less-than-virtuous behavior, and how He used them to further His work, we realize more than ever that God patiently and lovingly works with us too. Despite our shortcomings and outright sinfulness, He works to help us accomplish the purpose for which He created us. We must offer ourselves to Him every day to use as He sees fit, and work diligently, trusting that the results have a gainful effect upon that purpose. I admit, as a child, I was afraid to ask Him to use me as He would, because I felt that those who served God in foreign countries were really the true Christians, and I feared He might send me to some place in Africa or some other foreboding place! I didn't realize that we can serve Him in whatever field we choose. He has given us different talents so we can serve in many ways and places. (What a relief!!) Each one of us was created by Him for a part in His Plan. Some who are uneducated or who never left the place where they were born, feel inadequate and like they have failed because they never accomplished what others have. That is wrong. Just as each part of our body was made for a different function, and is equally important to our health, so is each person, with different talents, important to God's Plan for the world. In our culture today, the emphasis is put on the work which brings about wealth and success, but for those who are caregivers—both of people, and homes—there is little said. When they go quietly about their work and are unnoticed, they may wonder if anyone cares. God certainly does. We're directed in I Peter 4:8–10 that we are to be hospitable and comfort one another and to be good stewards of the gifts God has given us. In Romans 12:20, it even goes so far as to say we need to minister to our "enemies." What would the world be if all did the same work, or had the same likes and dislikes, same temperament, etc? He knows our weaknesses and even when we fail to do His will, He makes it come out for good to bring about His Plan. Even though we have no idea what part we play in that plan, we can trust from our past experience as Christians that it is better than we could plan for ourselves.

A More Abundant Life

We read that our needs are already known by God before we ask for them (Matt. 6:8), but if we ask they will be given (Matt. 7:7). We also read that Jesus said he came in order for us to have life and have it more abundantly (John 10:10).

When I think of all the blessings I have—despite my unworthiness—and added to that, the "more abundance," it's enough to bend the knee and bow the head in worship!

There are numerous things I can count as "abundance" in my life. One simple item was the recent acquiring of a list of references where one should look in the Bible for help when we feel lonely, rejected by friends, in despair, planning the budget, when we're sick, in a crisis, planning a trip, etc. What makes it add "abundance" to my life is that it is an aging, discolored piece of paper written in pencil by my mother. When it came in the mail from her sister, it was as if I had received a personal letter from my mom after she'd been gone for more than forty-five years. While it's not something I knew about, or needed for survival, God knew it would make me happy, and it guides me in finding help for things which come up in my life.

There are many times our lives are made "abundant"—when, in addition to those things we consider "necessary"—there are bonuses that bring unexpected pleasure. That was the case when my father revealed the story of my mother's missing engagement ring and gave it to me.

Such unexpected pleasure also comes when, after petitioning God for something, we realize that not only was the prayer answered, but in an even better way than that for which we had hoped.

Do too many of us take our lives for granted instead of realizing that each life has meaning and purpose? There are those whose goal is happiness and pleasure for themselves, and they scoff at people who take life "seriously." They don't seem to understand that happiness should come as a fringe benefit, or by-product, of the work they do. That goal is as wrong as when one decides to find "love." The love is gained as a result of giving of one's self to make another person happy—putting that person's happiness above your own, without thought of reward.

Where God put me to live and the one He gave to live with me is, indeed, a life more abundant than I could have asked for. When I hear about all the problems that people have when they live near the beach, lake, or where there are more floods, storms taking lives and homes, and other "natural disasters" but where affluent people choose to live,

I only feel sorry for them and am more thankful that God helped us to choose the mountains, and a more "out in the country" location. When I can go out and pick wild berries, flowers, see wild turkeys with their little chicks, or deer with their spotted fawn, squirrels running about and sights others only see in pictures; and have no close neighbors, have space to walk for exercise without having to dress a certain way or beat the sidewalks, I am glad we did not have a budget to afford that "luxury" to live in those places. There is peace here that my husband and I never would have found if we had gone out somewhere in search of such a place. God gave us what He knew would serve our purpose for all the changes that would come about in our family—covering more than fifty years.

Even greater than location, is the reality of the husband God provided with whom I could share my life. Despite all the difficulties we shared, I know I have accomplished more and had more happiness than would have been possible without him. (I hope the feeling has been mutual.) Certainly I always prayed for God to help me make the right choice in a lifetime partner just as I prayed He would help me choose, and prepare for, the right vocation, and help me carry out my purpose in life. Abundance has also resulted from being a mother and grandmother, and the opportunity to see the world anew through the eyes of children.

There was a time in my married life when I became aware, as never before, what is truly of value to me. It became necessary for us to leave the home in which we had lived since we were married, about five years before. We would have to move sixteen miles away and live over the funeral home. On the day we had gotten everything out of the house and on its way to the new location, I walked alone through the house we had enjoyed so much—and had been built according to the design my husband had drawn—and was feeling so sad. Then it came like a "bolt out of the blue," what had made this place so special: living here with the man I so truly loved, and I realized that I still had him, wherever we lived. It made it much easier. As God would have it, things worked out so that one year later we moved back to that house, put everything back where it had been, except for one special addition: our first child, a sweet, healthy baby girl.

Many people divide their lives into compartments. "Religion" is one part and has nothing to do with "business." We must, instead, so intermingle our "religion" with daily duties in our business or profession, and home, making us Christ-like through and through. If we do separate them, then those who reject Christianity—on the grounds that we are one way at church and a different person 24 hours later, at home or at work—would be justified in calling us "hypocrites."

Our thoughts must be guided by God so that regardless of where we are, we carry out God's will. To quote John Ruskin:

> "There is no action so slight nor so mean but it may be done to a great purpose, and ennobled therefore; nor is any purpose so great but that slight actions may help it, and may be done as to help it much, most especially, that chief of all purposes—the

> pleasing of God." Another bit, along the same line, which I have read, says: "I would give nothing for the man's religion whose very dog is not better off because of it." That's just another way of saying that to be a Christian is to be so permeated with His spirit that it "colors" everything we do no matter in what situation we are.

When some are asked to help with a cause that would help many people, they sometimes say they can't do it because they put their church first and don't have time to help—acting as if the only Christian work is attending church. While that is certainly valuable to each of us, it is easy to be a Christian while sitting in church—the difficulties come when we step outside and have to work in the real, less-than-ideal world. In some businesses the work must also be done on the Sabbath as well as every other day. In our funeral business it required someone to be there all the time and in my profession as a nurse, the hospital needs that service every day as well as 24 hours a day. If my husband went to church every Sunday, it meant that another employee had to be on "duty," so that would be selfish, and not the way God expects us to be. In the hospital, there have to be nurses there all the time to meet the needs of the sick. Even when the sick is not in a facility, the need is there 24 hours a day, seven days a week. The story of the good Samaritan comes to mind that the one along the roadside was ignored by those who thought their duties were more urgent than stopping to help someone in need. Of course, there are other businesses and professions which call for missing church services, but we all need that worship service, and re-fueling ourselves, as often as possible.

Females are so blessed these days to have the opportunity to either work outside the home or stay at home and be fulltime homemakers or mothers. There is value in whichever the woman chooses, just as it is for males if the situation allows. There is also no problem with a person who changes jobs often, even though that person may be criticized by those who work for years in the same employment. The person who chooses to work at the same place for a relatively short time, may have special talents as "change agents" or "catalysts" and are used to make changes or bring into existence a whole new entity. These people usually are not the ones to receive rewards for staying at one job, or in one industry, for so many years, but they are servants of God just as valuable as the "holders-on." God gives us all our talents and opportunities for using them as He intends. He, not us, is the judge of each one. "—The duties of home are a discipline for the ministries of heaven," says H.E. Manning. Discipline is very important in obeying God's will and carrying out duties, both great and small. We must never forget that those who do great things (and may receive great fame) usually have someone behind them who has given them great support and done the many "little things" that enabled them to accomplish the "big things." Perhaps those behind the scene will receive their reward in Heaven, as we know God sees and knows all things. Aren't we glad He is our judge, and not earthly beings?

Just as we must have the right motives in what we do,

we must also never forget that we need to make sure the causes we support with our money and time, are not using our gifts for purposes which go against our basic beliefs. We should always know the goals and objectives of organizations, and affiliations, before we join them or pledge our support. That money goes for the accomplishment of those goals and objectives. Even churches and other religious organizations that must send a portion of their collections to the national—or worldwide—headquarters need to scrutinize the use of that money. We have all had our eyes opened as never before—to schemes used in the name of religion or a good cause. Many greedy pockets have been lined with money collected purportedly to help certain diseases and those in dire need. We need also to decide whether it is right with God to spend large amounts of money to build a beautiful edifice for worship, or better serve His purpose by removing the ugly problems outside the church. God holds each person accountable for his/her actions or inactions whether he is alone or bolstered by a crowd. Some would put their consciences on hold and obediently follow the dictates of the leaders of the alliances they join, and allow the leaders to speak for them. The reality of the matter, of course, is that not only the one allowing another to act on his behalf, but also the one "acting," will have to defend himself (alone) to God. Reality number two is that when we are endowed with knowledge and are in places of influence, we are held more responsible than if we act in ignorance (Luke 12:42–48).

In summary, it seems to come down to tying all things in life to God's Plan in which every person on earth is created for a purpose. We must supply the action, and serve in ways that will carry out God's will even if it is counter to our own. We must be on God's side, instead of asking Him to be on ours, and to bless what we choose to do. If we want to please God, then we will have no will but His. If we each use the talents God gives us to accomplish that purpose, in whatever situation we daily find ourselves, then the problems of interpersonal relations; marriage; church; education; governments in counties, cities and nations would be solved. Since God really works through individuals, and it is the individuals who make up all those afore-mentioned entities, if each person sought only to do God's will, the outcome would be that God's purpose would be accomplished. We must have faith that God is not only there to guide us, and help us overcome the obstacles as we try to obey His will, but He will hold us accountable when we stray. That is the spiritual force which should tie together all the parts of each life, and therefore all parts of the universe.

We can't lightly discount those "out of the ordinary" things that happen. They may be messages from God that there's more work to do, or they may be "added abundance" to what we already have.

Power of Prayer

URING MANY TIMES IN my life I have been shown the power of prayer. Of course, to see its power, it must then be true that God answers prayer. It also goes back to the motive—or reason—we're praying, and our sincerity. If we pray for selfish reasons or for something not good for us, God will hear us, but the answer may be "no." If we are not truly sincere in what we ask, we may not get the answer we want, and if we ask for forgiveness, but are unforgiving to others, the answer, again, may not give us what we ask.

As related previously about my father improving enough to come home after being institutionalized for seventeen years, that was truly the power of prayer. Not only had my mother prayed for his recovery, but I prayed daily along with her and for all the years from her death in 1944 until he came home in 1955. I feel sure there were others praying for him too.

After my husband of 78 suffered a devastating stroke which paralyzed his left side, prayer became a constant with me. Even in this worst of all times, God had mercy and didn't take him, but "conditioned" me to the time when I would be left alone. While mowing the lawn with a riding mower which stalled on a hillside, he was knocked down by it when he got off to check it. When I got to him, I saw he had suffered a stroke, and got an ambulance. While he was in the emergency room (which seemed like hours), I was on my knees in the rest room praying for God to help him.

The doctor told me that if the scan showed that he had suffered a stroke, I would have to make a quick decision as to whether he should have a medication to dissolve the clot or whether not to give it. He warned me of the risks either way. Again, God helped me when it was found that instead of a clot, it was bleeding on the brain, so the only decision necessary was to decide where he would be taken for treatment. Since my husband had never lost consciousness, he was able to help me decide where he wanted to be treated. It was about 8 p.m. and there seemed to be an impending storm, so the doctor said it was somewhat doubtful if the hospital in Charlottesville could send a helicopter, but they said they could. He was flown by helicopter, and I was able to get his sister to drive me there, three hours away. I had left a message for my son in Atlanta, and he had called the hospital so I was able to talk with him. My husband was in intensive care and was responsive and talkative as well as cheerful. I was able to stay in the lounge nearby and check on him during the night, and my sister-in-law stayed nearby in a motel. He continued to amaze the nurses and me with his cheerfulness the next day, and even asked me to turn on television that night to watch the Gaither program, as he could see a clock nearby and it was the time we usually watched it at home. We enjoyed it together.

He worsened on Sunday night after being moved from intensive care, and I feared he would not live until our son could get there. Again, the next day he surprised us and was joking about everyone working for the different therapies and told our son when he arrived, that he "thought they were going to kill me before you got here." By midweek, they transferred him to a hospital in our state where he could get therapy and he was terribly discouraged because he thought he could come home instead. The therapists there were very helpful to him, but it was about seventy miles from our home. I was not able to go every day to see him, but went every other day and stayed overnight on weekends when there were less activities for him.

As a Registered Nurse of more than fifty years, I had such fears about what was happening and the prognosis. We also had been married for more than fifty years so I felt as "one" with him and didn't hesitate to question his medical and nursing care. I prayed for guidance to make the right decisions and for alertness in all matters of care, as well as for the right doctors, therapists, and all who had to do with his care. I also prayed that I would be where I should be, do what I should do, say what I should say and hold my tongue where I should hold my tongue. My husband wanted me with him all the time, and when I would explain what had to be done, he would tell me it was alright as long as I said so. That's a wonderful love and trust, but made me feel so terribly responsible. There was only the two of us.

Through the months of his illness, he was in four different facilities, and I traveled many miles back and forth but God helped me through it all and let me know what it was like to be at home alone, learning to do the things my husband had always taken care of in years past. I thanked Him for that training and guidance. Of course, there were many ups and downs during that time.

It was better for me when I was with him than when I was home. My nursing skills came in well as he needed more care than staff could provide. It certainly was a learning experience when the tables were turned and I saw medical care on the receiving side. Like anything else, there are those with whom you are happy and feel secure when they are there to provide care for a loved one, and those whom you wish were not there. Sometimes I was shown respect and they appreciated my help, and sometimes I was not. In the years when I was a Nursing Instructor, I always taught students to treat a patient as they would want the dearest person in their life treated. I found "the dearest person" had more effect than to say "the way you would want to be treated." Some would respond, they didn't mind if they were exposed, but would admit they wouldn't want their mother or spouse exposed indignantly. Members of the family should be treated the same way because I learned, more than ever before, how great the stress is upon the loved ones.

By praying for the right ones to give him care, I felt much more secure and when I saw no progress, I would pray that they would be shown a better way, or a more effective person would be there. He often would rebel at therapy so I would pray for him to have less discomfort and be more accepting, as well as for him to feel more encouragement. It was so difficult to see a deeply Christian, active man, so depressed he didn't think the effort was worth it. Being patient, and understanding the change in one you've known for so long, took much prayer, but I must admit that I failed many times. It was so hard to understand he was so truly weak. We deny to ourselves that this is happening to the one we love and have seen as such a different person all the past years. We want to think they just have to work harder at it, and they will get back to where they were before this happened. We mourn the loss of the person we have always known, even before we lose them to death.

It was most difficult when he wanted to come home and I would have to tell him he had to get much better before I could get the care to help me with him at home.

I was shown as never before, how God comes through for us when we are so in need, when a doctor told me to come to his office to talk with him as I insisted I could bring him home and manage. It was late in the evening, and I had to drive at least 69 miles and didn't see well to drive at night. He explained in the kindest way he could that I had been misled at the hospital where he had been admitted after the brain hemorrhage. Although the neurosurgeon had told me my husband would recover his ability to walk, at least with assistance, and be able to eat, instead of being tube fed, this Clinical Psychologist, after thoroughly working with my husband, said the brain damage was greater than I had been told. He told me I had lost him as the way I had known him to be, and he would never be the same. He said I must get him in a nursing home (which my husband and I had agreed we wouldn't want) at least until he improved more. It had been only 5–6 weeks since the stroke, so he said I was neither emotionally nor physically able to care for him. He made me realize that it would be unfair to my husband as well as me, because he needed more therapy and training to better help himself.

I was completely devastated to learn that discouraging news. As I drove that distance, I prayed and cried. As soon as I got home, I was down on my knees asking God's help and guidance. What could I do? Nursing homes were all so expensive and where could he get the therapy he needed? At the hospital it took about 3 people to get him from bed to wheelchair. I really felt the need to talk to someone, but it was our son's wedding anniversary and I didn't want to spoil the occasion. Actually, I knew I was too upset to talk to anyone but God, as only He knew what I was feeling and trying to consider, regarding my husband's feelings and situation.

Finally, after some sleep, I awoke feeling the urgency to get to the task of learning about which nursing homes had the best therapists, what the costs would be, what services would be provided, and where a bed was available. All these concerns were again taken to God. Several nurses had told me problems about conditions where they worked, and it seemed they were in all the nursing homes—and hospitals. I felt I could handle the "nursing care," however, so the main concern was to get the therapists who could best meet his needs so he could improve enough for me to bring him home.

Although I heard the best therapists were in one facility, it turned out that he couldn't get in there. Prayer was continuous. An opening was available at a nursing home only nine miles from our home, and the therapists, reputedly, were very good. While it was understaffed with nurses and Aides—as were all the others—they were very caring, patient, and respectful to both him and me. Everyone there, in all departments, was concerned and caring, from administration to housekeeping and maintenance. Many knew us personally since he had been a kind and caring undertaker and had dealt with them when they had deaths in their families, or they knew me.

The power of prayer was evident to me in both large and small matters. When expenses were taking their toll and he seemed to be at a standstill in therapy and began to be more depressed, someone mentioned the possibility of going to the Veterans' Administration hospital about fifty miles away. Again, I didn't know whether that would be a good change or not.

Since he kept complaining of so much pain in his left hip, on which he had fallen when he had the stroke, the doctor decided to have it x-rayed (although it had been x-rayed at the time he was taken to the hospital, and showed no fracture). He was taken by ambulance to an orthopedic surgeon a few miles away, and the x-ray again showed no fracture. Since I had known the physician previously and trusted him completely, I told him of the situation and that I was considering moving him to the V.A. facility, but didn't know whether that was best for him. He told me to talk it over with my husband and to "pray about it" and make my decision based on that. To get such advice from a physician was unusual for me, but it was certainly not disappointing advice for me.

As I prayed, doors seemed to open to make me aware God was still working to help me. There was a qualifying evaluation that he had to meet to be admitted for therapy in the Veterans' Hospital, since his illness was not "service connected." The stroke was not a result of his serving in the military in World War II. He met the requirements that said he was potentially capable of rehabilitation and was given six free months in the hospital. There, of course, were many changes requiring adjustments and adapting to the personnel. I had hoped he would be inspired by other military personnel who were there for similar treatment, to put forth more effort in therapy, but it didn't happen. I was not allowed to be with him in therapy as I had been (and was even encouraged to be there) in the other facilities. He had sometimes worked to please me and would want to show me what he had accomplished. He was very lethargic much of the time, and then he had a severe attack of bleeding from the bladder—a result of the weakness caused by radiation he had a year earlier for prostate cancer—which prevented his being able for some weeks to take the therapy.

Finally it was decided he had no "potential" for rehabilitation because he was not progressing in therapy. I was suddenly told that I must either take him home or to a nursing home. This, again, was sudden and devastating news. He, of course, had been unable to progress in being rehabilitated as he had the setbacks as well as the depression, which made him feel the difficulty and pain of the therapeutic exercises weren't worth it. Although I told them I was unable to care for him at home and could not afford a nursing home, I was told I had a month to move him.

Again, my prayers were answered when the wife of a patient in my husband's room told me she had gone through this, and I needed to contact our Representative in Congress. This I did, and in not too long a time I received a letter from the Director of the hospital that said he would not be discharged because of a deterioration of his condition. There were also times when I had to do "battle" with doctors, nurses and other caregivers, and I was always asking for God's guidance in what I should say or do, and I felt very secure that my prayers were answered—sometimes in very surprising ways.

Holidays (especially Christmas) were times I dreaded most. We would always agree that the next year would be better and he would be home. At Thanksgiving, I was able to take some foods he liked and we were able to eat together, with me feeding him a little.

Christmas was very difficult with all the merriment, hearing others' plans and remembering our past happy times. The weather got very bad the Christmas he was at the Veterans' hospital, but I arose very early, baked a turkey with all the trimmings, and took gifts. He only ate a few bites before he had to be put to bed because of the pain of bladder spasms. As the day wore on, the snow piled up and I knew I could not drive the 50 miles home. I had a cousin who lived nearby, and I had always gone there if I couldn't leave him to come home, but she was stranded at her parent's home several miles away.

The hospital personnel were kind enough to move him to a private room where I could use a cot to stay all night. The very bumpy, unwieldy cot was nothing compared to the happiness of my being able to stay with him instead of coming back to a very lonely home on Christmas evening, which I had so greatly dreaded. God works in such amazing ways to show us His concern. Again, beyond my wildest imagination, the next morning my husband awakened bright and cheerful and feeling much better. They got him up in a wheelchair after I bathed him, and I got him into the bathroom to help him shave. When he returned from therapy, the therapist joked that he had told my husband I'd better bring him turkey every day if that's what made him "work out" as well as he did. What a happy day it turned out to be, so that the dread I had had and all my depressed feelings were turned inside out when the snow came to keep me with him. I had "asked," "sought," and "knocked" and God truly opened the door to show His love for me and allow us to be together. All things, including the snow, had worked together for my (and my husband's) good. It was much easier to come home the evening following Christmas than it would have been the day of Christmas.

After he had been there about five months, I began to have a very strong feeling that I must bring him home. When I would mention it to anyone, I was told there was no way for me to ever think I could take care of him at home. One doctor said that for me to ever think I could take care of him at home was "unrealistic;" nurses and Aides caring for him would tell me it was impossible. I began to ask at the hospital what help, in the way of equipment, and services could they provide. "Where are you going to find people who will come in to help at home?" They would remind me of the costliness *if* I could find them. These were all legitimate questions because after coordinating a support group for about 10 years, for families of Alzheimer patients, I had heard family members seeking answers to the same questions. Somehow, I felt sure of my response to those who questioned me, when I would say "I don't know the answers right now, but I know they will come."

As it turned out, the V.A. loaned hospital equipment, such as bed, wheelchair, electronic lift, feeding pump and several other essentials. Many supplies and medications were provided at a discount since he was a veteran of World War II. When I started looking for those I needed to help me care for him, there too, God provided a very competent, skilled worker whose father had been a very good friend of my husband, as well as her grandfather who had been a minister. She was Afro-American, very cheerful and often would sing and have him join in. On some mornings when she came to bathe him, she would sing "Good morning to you, good morning to you. We're all in our places, with sunshiny faces and this is the way to start a new day," and soon had him joining in and sometimes, he would even start it before she would. She was very good for him and he would try to cooperate with her. (He had a local preacher's license and had served in many churches when ministers were on vacation, and in one Afro-American church, for over a year when they were unable to employ a minister. Therefore, he and this lady would often discuss—in his presently limited way—religious subjects. She was attending college part-time, and he would encourage and praise her when she told him of her good grades. He was pleased she was pursuing her education in middle age and at the local college he had worked very hard to get established here. (Through the years he had been concerned that many in this area had to go a distance to get their education, so worked for years, even with legislators, to get this one started.) The V.A. also provided a caregiver who could help not only to care for my husband but also do some household chores. It was much more than I ever expected, and he had been overjoyed when he heard he would finally, after twenty-two months, be able to come home. He needed to continue his therapy, so a very competent Physical Therapist came for a limited time and taught how we must work with him. He was very unhappy at that and it was very difficult, but we worked with him in doing the necessary exercises and got him up with the help of the lift and had him sitting outside in the wheelchair. He was so pleased with all who helped him, and participated in some activities with them.

God was so good to let our son, his wife and two little girls, aged 3 and 4 ½, come to visit us for Father's Day at the hospital, a few weeks before he came home in July. They drew pictures and showed their love for him as they played around him, to his delight. Fortunately we had visited them in their Atlanta home in May, 2002, before his stroke in August, so we had those happy memories. The oldest one, who loves to draw, and does a good job, made a picture of her granddad and me in the yard holding hands, in front of their house, under a shiny sun, very detailed, and I had kept it on the bulletin boards in his rooms in the different facilities where he was treated. It and other drawings were brought home to also decorate the walls in our bedroom at home.

Of course, when he came home, there was another big problem to solve—money to pay for his care at home. We had been allowed six months in the V.A. hospital before we were charged for his care. Although he was a veteran who had served overseas, since his disability was not service connected, we had to pay for the six weeks beyond the six months free stay. Anyone who has had to have health care, especially in nursing homes, is aware of the alarmingly high costs. The power of prayer continued to work. When I asked for guidance in how to pay for care at home, it came to me that I could sell some of our property in the back of our lot which we had held onto. I explained to my husband why it was necessary to now sell a few acres of our seventeen, and he understood and agreed. I was shown how to put the money to its best use.

As we had hoped, we were able to spend our 52nd wedding anniversary, Thanksgiving, and Christmas at home. He helped the caregiver and me to decorate a little Christmas tree in the dining room (where we had formerly had a large tree that he had helped decorate) and from bed he enjoyed the blinking lights on a little tree in our bedroom. The helper who was there during the day helped him plan a surprise gift for me. She even guided his right hand (as his dominant left hand was paralyzed) to sign a card she had selected for him to give me. She was truly a special gift to us from God.

A few days before Christmas, however, he became less responsive. We still got him up, but he talked much less and answered less. I wasn't sure he would last through the night sometimes. When we received the gifts from our son and his family, he was aware and looked at some pictures of the family. On Christmas I didn't call anyone to help me. I got him up myself and had him at the table as I ate our usual turkey dinner. He was unable to eat any. I opened the packages and told him what they were, and from whom, but he kept his eyes closed. God enabled me to get him back to bed with the lift, as I didn't want to bother others on that day, although I'd been told to call.

He kept going "down hill" and on the 30th he died. The girl provided by the V.A.—who had helped him prepare for Christmas (and had become like family) was there with us. He kept holding on, and I was able to do what I never thought I could—pray that he would be out of his misery and go on to be with God. I also let him know I would be alright (although it was so difficult to say that) and it was alright to go on to be with God and see the parents he loved. He had so greatly missed his beloved father with whom he had worked at the funeral home before his death from a stroke almost fifty years before.

He had written out all his funeral arrangements thirteen years before, including which funeral home he wanted, the casket, the minister, pall bearers, songs, readings, and clothing he wanted used. I had never seen the arrangements as I never wanted to think of a time I would have to live without him. I had always prayed that I would never live beyond him, but knew I didn't want him to have to live in the condition in which he was.

I felt I had been so blessed to have been married to a husband so loving, patient, and understanding for fifty-two years. There had been many difficult times that God had brought us through and kept us together. We both had been very thankful for that. We felt God had put us together and guided us to accomplish the purpose He had for us as a "team," and as individuals, in helping people and being happy while doing it. I continue to feel I would not have been anything worthwhile without him beside me encouraging me all the way. (He bolstered me and gave me a higher self esteem than I ever had—or feel I would have had. He gave me the secure feeling I had never had, and never gave me reason to doubt his love.) He also was an unusually considerate husband in doing work the wife usually does, so I could work at my "project," or study for my college classes, or whatever was "pressing" upon me. He valued my work and ambitions, as he did his. He served as a good role model as husband and father, and I see it in our son today as he is an unusual husband, helping in all things as he saw his dad doing and as a loving, patient father, husband, and good provider.

That night alone, after he had been taken to the funeral home, was difficult, and yet I knew God was with me and was helping me to accept it. God had really been gracious to me in having "conditioned" me to losing him.

I see the great power of prayer in all that "saddest of all times in my life," and continue to see it in the almost two years since his death. Each morning before I get out of bed,

I pray that God will use me to be accessible to others who need me and to help me accomplish the purpose for which He left me on this earth in a new way of life—alone. I have had to face surgery three times since living alone, and have always asked for prayers from my friends and family to help me through it, and have done remarkably well with each. Close friends have stayed with me during the surgery and as needed when I came home. I prayed for the best physicians, health care providers, hospitals, and therapists to do the work necessary and felt very trusting that He had given me that, so I didn't worry. I followed instructions since I knew they were being guided by God, in answer to my (and others') prayers. It is unreasonable to ask God for healing and then fail to follow good rules for health, and instructions given by those whom you are paying to help you. Health is very dependent on guidance from God and we need good health to be able to help those who are less fortunate and unable to do things for themselves. The Scripture makes it very clear that we are to do to others what we would have them to do for us, and to be merciful to others, and we will receive mercy.

The first Sunday after my son left for his home in Atlanta, I went to the Afro-American church where my husband had filled in as pastor for the long time they were unable to employ one, and where they were his friends. One of the members, a long time friend, had written and delivered the eulogy for his funeral, and it was not only very touching but gave great tribute to him. The Sunday service, and friendliness, were good for me, and the choir (which had sung at my husband's funeral) was, as always, joyful in worship, and I told the congregation how much they had meant to him and me through the years. (Our children had also enjoyed that church, especially the music, when they had attended with us.)

The next Sunday I attended the Sunday School class in the Methodist Church to which we had belonged for so many years (and at which I had been a Kindergarten teacher in Sunday School for over ten years, both before and after our children were born. My husband had also taught a young people's class there in earlier years.) That class had shown its concerns for us both and sent cards and Christmas gifts to my husband all the time of his illness. I wanted to thank them and was so welcomed that I have attended it, as well as church, ever since. With an invitation to substitute for one of the teachers one Sunday and then to become one of the regular teachers, I decided, after prayer, to take them up on it. It has really been very helpful to me, and it is always a learning experience when we teach and try to find answers for others with questions. This, I feel very surely, was an answer to my prayer to help me be useful in God's work, and my prayer to let me use each minute of the day in accordance with His will. We need His guidance in the use of our time, money, and other resources, as He would have us use them. There are so many decisions to make and so many options, and when we have no earthly soul to help us with those decisions, it is especially difficult. Another help, I feel, has been the ministers who have been at the church I attend. There have been so many different learning experiences. Now when problems come up with the car, the furnace, insurance, taxes, etc, I have to find how to take care of them where he had always attended to those matters. I have had the help of friends to overcome the lonely times, and even when it seems there are so many things to keep up with, I realize that they, too, are "gifts" for which to be thankful as it means I don't have time to feel so lonely, and it also means God is helping me to maintain my home by making it easier to live in the same place where our whole family lived together. That is important, to live where our "roots have been planted" with our loved ones. It seems like my husband's spirit is near me in this place where we lived so long and raised our two children. It would be very difficult, I think, to lose my loved one and also the home we shared, and have to make an adjustment to a new home as well as a new way of life alone. Since he and I dated for six years before marrying, it seems like there was little of my life without him. We did not marry until I finished my nursing program of three years, and before that I was in high school for three years. He was in the Marines when we started dating, and while I was in nursing, he was in college for two years and then in embalming college. We dated mostly by phone while he was in his schools and I, in mine. His father jokingly said he was glad we were getting married as his phone bill would go down. When he was not in school he was helping his father in the funeral home. I was at a distance in my school and as I affiliated with other hospitals for my clinical experiences—three months at St. Elizabeth's in Washington, DC for psychiatry, and six months at the University of Virginia, Charlottesville, for obstetrics and pediatrics. It did afford us the joy of visiting many places of interest in those areas when he could visit me for the brief times I had off—or he did, as his father kept him very busy. These are memories I cherish. They are another gift from God—memories. I pray I will always have my memories of the past with my husband and family, and that they will help me to be a better follower of God. Again, it shows how God continuously blesses our lives despite the many times we have disappointed Him.

Another belief I have is that God prepares us for the life He knows we need to accomplish the purpose for which He created us. Some things happened in my life which make me feel my calling was to be a nurse and also the wife of an undertaker. Many have asked how one could live over the funeral home and be what is necessary when in a profession where one has to work with those who have died, as well as with families dealing with death.

My mother worked to clean the funeral home of the grandfather and father of the one who later became my husband. On Saturdays, it was necessary for me, about ten or eleven, to go with her to work. The son of the undertaker who lived in the funeral home was a little younger than I, so he and I would play around the funeral home—often "hide and seek." He was actually a little less "brave" than I, so I knew if I hid in the room upstairs where the caskets were, that it would take him awhile to find me. One time I crawled back in a corner where the casket was sitting diagonally from wall to wall, and I had plenty of space to sit. I waited such a long time and he never came, so I crawled out and along in front of the caskets until I came to the door, when it suddenly opened, and expecting it to be my friend, I jumped up and yelled "Boo!" Only, it wasn't my friend, but his father with some people to see the caskets to make a selection. I dashed down the stairs and went to find my friend, who was in their apartment, going about his play. Needless to say, my mother was very embarrassed for my behavior, and I had some apologizing to do. By spending some of my time in a funeral home in that way, I never had any problem with living in a funeral home for the year my husband and I had to do so, later in life. There was no problem, also, as I helped with doing cosmetics and hair of females who had died. As a nurse, I also often helped my patients by "doing" their hair, as it meant they were feeling better. We often said that when men wanted to be shaved and women wanted their makeup on and hair fixed, they were getting better.

Another experience which helped me decide I wanted to be a nurse came when I was about eleven and my mother had to have a thyroidectomy. Since there were only the two of us, I was very uneasy about the surgery and whether she would survive. I prayed very hard for God to let her get along well and live in good health. I promised Him that if He would let her live, that I would never talk back to her, or "sass" her as I had done. She got along well, and I certainly thanked Him but learned a lesson: that even with our good intentions to keep promises, we do not always keep them when we are tested. I also learned as I matured, that we do not "bargain" with God. Despite all that, He answered my prayers. During that time, also, He took good care of me as well as her. The surgeon was very kind as well as skilled in this type of surgery. Since I had been with her when she had gone for examinations, he knew our situation, and he knew I wanted—at that early age—to be a nurse. He directed the nurses to let me sleep down the hall from my mother in an empty room. When a patient came for it, he had them prepare me a place to sleep in her room, in a chair. I helped her with all I could, and won praise from the nurses. It was good preparation for my life to come. In those days a patient who had had the thyroid removed was kept in bed, and the head was kept from moving for a time following surgery. She was there for at least a week, as was the custom for surgeries in "those days." I really enjoyed helping my mother and the nurses. Again, I learned that God answers prayers, and later realized that it was all a part of God's Plan for me.

Is it possible that our loved ones who have gone before us are still with us in Spirit? It seems at times that they are very close and may be helping God to watch over us. I know that I want never to dishonor my husband or his memory. Hebrews 12:1 tells us of a "great cloud of witnesses" who "compass about" us, and I get encouragement from a devotion I read which says we should never be lonely or forsaken in this life, and asks how they can forget us or love us less because they are made perfect and have the power to love us more. It asks if we remember them, then will they not also remember us with God. It goes on to say that nothing can separate us from the Communion of Saints. That is a great comfort to me.

So Be It

$\mathcal{S}$OMETIMES, I HAVE learned, we ask for something and God answers our prayers, but we seem to fight Him all the way. When I realized that I was not keeping up with medications, as I wanted to as a Nurse, I asked God to help me to learn more about them. I found myself employed as a Clinical Instructor in a nursing school, with students to supervise during their education to work at the bedside of patients in the hospital. A part of their experience, of course, was to give medications to patients. They were assigned to a certain number of patients and had to check their charts as to medications they would have to administer, and before they could give them they must know several things about the medicine. They had to prepare a card with the information on it so they could refer to it when necessary. Of course, I, too, had to learn the same things so I could question them—but I had to do that for each student—so I found myself learning about medicines (as I had asked God to help me do) but it was a lot of work. Again I learned that we can ask for things but we often have to work to make it happen. It was good discipline.

I want to learn more about the Bible and scriptures which I can refer to when I need help, but God will not just hand that knowledge to me. I must study the Bible more, seek other means to add to that, such as go to Bible study groups, read other sources of information, and attend church and Sunday School. God works with us, but expects us to put forth effort also. As we are told in 2 Thessalonians 3:10, "… If anyone will not work, let him not eat," then it should be the same for learning. If we are not interested enough to put out the effort, then we cannot expect to learn. I think we also appreciate more those things we feel we have earned by our own work.

We often see things in retrospect that we are unable to see at the time. There was a time when it seemed we would lose the funeral business my husband had established. We prayed for guidance and help for business to improve and he tried to save it, but it seemed as if it wouldn't survive. We prayed and worked to get a buyer, but in the meantime my husband decided he would get education to become a teacher, and took classes in college to prepare him. We both took classes, in fact. Then as time passed and no buyer came, the business started picking up, and we were able not only to continue, but see an increase. He greatly believed his father had run his business in a Christian way and never believed in overselling to people when they may have bought more than they could afford, only to have to go in debt for years because of being pressured at a time they were most vulnerable. He always said he wanted to treat others as he would want his wife treated if the role were reversed. My husband conducted his business the same way. We decided that God intended him to continue in the funeral business so people would have more options in funeral homes. We never regretted that decision, and our business provided us with our needs, though not affluence. His goal was to fulfill the purpose for which he thought he was created and to carry on a business of which his father would approve. I have always felt very honored and proud that I had the privilege to be of help to him, as he was to me.

Faith is so necessary and such a help to us when difficult times come up. How very hard it would be if my mother had not taught me about prayer and faith in God. It would also be bad if one would love another who did not share the belief in prayer and faith. God spared both my husband and me that unhappiness. We tried to pass it on to our children and to model Christianity and take them to Sunday School and church. We prayed with them at night, and had short devotions at breakfast. I recall the time I had to tell our little daughter (at 6 or 7) when I picked her up after school, that the elderly babysitter she and her brother had, had died. She began to cry and her brother (then 3 or 4 years old) told her not to worry, that they would see her again in Heaven. That's one of the times you feel so proud of your child, and feel surprised that he/she has picked up that belief and passed it on.

God allowed me to have joy again in the same way about a month after my husband died. My son's little 5 ½ year old daughter, who loves to draw and does very well at it, made a large picture of her granddad (whom she loved so much) as an angel up in heaven in a long sleeved striped shirt and wings, long hair and a beard (as Jesus is pictured) and me down below him, and she had her mother print the message: "Grandma, I'm sorry Granddad died and that you can't live with him any more, but you will see him again, Grandma." She signed her own name in big letters. She also drew a large heart with an arrow through it since it was for Valentine's Day. It was reminiscent of her father's beliefs at a young age. She also had sent with her father, when he came for his dad's funeral, a picture she had drawn for me, with her granddad up above the clouds looking down at her daddy and me side by side. The sun was shining and we all three had smiles on our faces. At a later date she told me that I would never be alone because God was always with me. "Out of the mouths of babes…"

Another recollection which witnesses to the power of prayer, and how God cares for us personally, concerns my father. After he had come home from the long stay in the hospital and was living in an apartment in a city near his childhood home, and about a three hour drive from where we lived, he seemed to be having some mental problems. Neighbors saw him doing strange things, nothing harmful, but somewhat disturbing, so had called the police. The son of my dad's brother was very close to my dad and would go to check on him, and usually by that time he seemed alright and would laugh off the incident. Once, however, the police had put him in jail for disturbance, so my cousin called me. My husband and I went to see what the problem was. I was so afraid he may have to be hospitalized again and didn't know how we could tell if it was digression to his former mental problems or something minor. He had a personality that would make him very outgoing and friendly when he liked someone but would just leave the room when someone was around he didn't like or know. He was sometimes very stubborn and may be argumentative. I feared he would be misjudged and hospitalized when not necessary. I prayed all the way that that would not happen, that there would be some way to determine correctly. There were three licensed physicians to determine his "sanity." They were very nice and seemed concerned. My dad was glad to see us but was completely disoriented as to time and situation. He thought he was back working on the railroad, and that they had found oil on his home property (which had natural gas in abundance, but no oil) and he would share with us and we would be well off. He was very happy. While it hurt to see him so disoriented, I realized God had answered my prayer that the right determination would be made. There was no doubt that he needed to be hospitalized. Fortunately, (and as God would have it) we were able to get him admitted to a long term Veterans' Administration hospital only about 2 hours from our home, in a unit for the elderly, and we, our children, could visit him easier than where he had formerly been for seventeen years. He was never able to come home again but was happy there and loved to receive brownies from home, and he would sometimes talk baseball with our son when we visited. He died at 92 and was able to be up and go to the dining area until shortly before his death—all a blessing. God was good to allow him to be home with us and enjoy his little grandchildren and the outdoors which he had so loved, and for that we are thankful. Our children were able to know the joy of grandparents—my father and my husband's mother—and they, to enjoy our children.

As I look back through the years and the times that I have felt very much alone and when, after my mother died (leaving me without any direct family members), I felt I didn't "belong" to anyone and missed that *personal* concern, and a return of that feeling of not really "belonging" to anyone since my husband died, I realize how great a gift my mother left me—teaching me about God and the power of prayer. He has given me so many blessings even as unworthy as I am, and so many kind, thoughtful friends, a lot of worthwhile things to work on and keep me busy, but there is still that sense of a part of me missing. As in Genesis 2:24, when we marry someone we become one, so I think it seems logical that when one dies the other one feels incomplete and at a loss. I feel very surely, however, by what I was taught by my mother, and what my husband and I both believed, that there is still a purpose for me without my husband, just as there was a purpose for me with him. We each had a purpose to fulfill with each other's love and support, and now there is still work ahead for me. The years with the mate God gave me only deepened my learning and faith in Him and the power of prayer—but having him beside me, loving me as no one else could, made my life more happy and contented and I surely will miss that. God has constantly shown me through all these years that He will never desert me and that He is right there for me to call upon for every need I feel I have. He has shown me, too, how "faith the size of a mustard seed" proves fruitful and that even when I fail Him, He never fails me. As I have written earlier, however, I know He will discipline me as we discipline those we love so that they know we care for them and want them to be more perfect in order to someday live in Heaven with God. Faith must enable us to accept whatever happens as the will of God, because there can be no failure if we have sincerely done our best in our efforts toward fulfilling our divine destiny. As it's been said, "If you do your best, the angels can't do better." Stated another way by F.W. Robertson: "No work truly done, no word earnestly spoken, no sacrifice freely made was ever made in vain."

Despite the faith we have, there are still many times when we wonder why things happen and what we are to do. We are comforted by Matthew 6:8: "Your Father knows the things you have need of before you ask Him," yet we wonder.

Besides the Scriptures, God provides us with friends who help us in so many ways and one close friend, with whom there is mutual trust, sent me what has helped me immeasurably in SO many situations and I have shared it with others who have questions:

There will be times when you will not see the immediate way ahead. You may be filled with panic, wanting to avoid what could be a disastrous step. Remember that you do not always need to see the road ahead. It is sufficient, for the moment, to see ME!

When the time is right for a choice to be made, you will know, and I will assist you through it. Until that time, be sure that merely keeping close to Me guarantees you're moving in the right direction, despite questions and doubts raging in your mind.

When you cannot see clearly the next step, there is good reason for My withholding that awareness. It becomes a time of trust-trust, very often that I will simply allow My wish for you to happen. Do not feel the awful responsibility of choosing your path when that is not necessary for the moment. Just hide in Me and know that you will soon see clearly. Until then, you are precisely where I want you to be.

("It Is Sufficient To See Me," excerpted from the devotional, *I Am With You*, by John Woolley.)

To know that the grave is not the end, and that there is life after death has always been a deep belief of both my husband and me, from experiences we have had in our lives, as well as Bible teachings. Second Timothy 1:10 tells us that "—our Savior Jesus Christ—abolished death and brought life and immortality to light through the gospel." Therefore, there need be no fear of death. For that I am grateful, and pray I can live a more godly life daily and witness for Him, to prove myself more worthy of the many blessings I have received. Another good thing we, as Christians know, is that He knows what I need even more than I do.

We must pray that those who do not know these things will learn them—and we must help as much as possible—so that they, too, will not be so devastated when they lose loved ones. Life, I feel, would be unbearable had I not been taught these things and been shown how easy it is to pray, making available a power to help control my life—regardless of where, or in what condition I am, or how inadequate I have been in my efforts to do God's will. I wonder if suicide is the result of that great despair one must feel if there is the belief that there is no power other than their own to solve their dilemma and that no one cares. I pray, in some way, this "witnessing" will help spread the word which we read over and over in many places in the Scriptures, that God is there for us and loves us so much He sent His son, Jesus, to show us the way, and he paid in full for our sins so that all we have to do is accept this gift and show our faith by living for Him. To do that we only need to Ask, Seek, and Knock in order to know how we can live a life for him. We will never cease to be amazed what power prayer has.

> Lord, I know not what I ought
> to ask of Thee; Thou
> only knowest what we need;
> Thou lovest me better
> than I know how to love
> myself. O Father: give to
> Thy child that which he himself
> knows not how to
> ask. I dare not ask either for crosses or
> consolations; I simply present
> myself before Thee; I open
> my heart to Thee. Behold my
> needs which I know not
> myself; see, and do according
> to Thy tender mercy.
> Smite, or heal; depress me, or
> raise me up; I adore all

Thy purposes without knowing them; I am silent; I offer myself in sacrifice: I yield myself to Thee; I would have no other desire than to accomplish Thy will. Teach me to pray; pray Thyself in me.

(Francois De La Mothe Fenelon)

References

The Interpreters Bible. New York Abingdon Press Nashville.

Tileston, Mary W. *Daily Strength for Daily Needs.* G. P. Putnam's Sons, New York, 1928.

Cruden, Alexander, *M.A. Cruden's Concordance of the Holy Scriptures.* Pyramid Publications, New York, New York.

Tate Publishing & *Enterprises*

Tate Publishing is committed to excellence in the publishing industry. Our staff of highly trained professionals, including editors, graphic designers, and marketing personnel, work together to produce the very finest books available. The company reflects the philosophy established by the founders, based on Psalms 68:11,

"THE LORD GAVE THE WORD AND GREAT WAS THE COMPANY OF THOSE WHO PUBLISHED IT."

If you would like further information, please call
1.888.361.9473
or visit our website
www.tatepublishing.com

Tate Publishing & *Enterprises*, LLC
127 E. Trade Center Terrace
Mustang, Oklahoma 73064 USA